Cloud Farm

Cloud Farm

High on Banks Peninsula

Jane Chetwynd

Longacre Press

Acknowledgements
Many people have encouraged and helped me in the writing of this book. For getting me started I must thank Janet Holst, Margaret Lovell-Smith, Anna Rogers and John Farnsworth. For encouragement along the way I thank Nedra Johnson, Sue Sky, Eileen Rennie, Wendy Logan, Denise Baldwin and Fiona Farrell. For reading early drafts my thanks to Helen Ford, Mollie Dickinson, John Chetwynd, Anne Chetwynd and Jane Seatter. For editorial help I am indebted to Penelope Todd and the team at Longacre Press. Finally, all my thanks go to Heather Chapman for her ongoing support and all that she has done to make Cloud Farm what it is today.

Photographs are reproduced courtesy of Bruce Gould (front cover), Cynthia Roberts (back cover), Denise Baldwin, Heather Chapman, Lisa Potts and Diana Rattray.

ISBN 1 877135 95 X

First published by Longacre Press, 2004
30 Moray Place, Dunedin, New Zealand

Reprinted 2004

Book and cover design by Christine Buess
Printed by Astra Print, Wellington, New Zealand

Contents

You must be mad... 7
Dreaming of escape 10
When dreams come to land 24
The day of the bonfires 35
A different way of looking at it 45
One brick at a time 53
The dreaded weed 65
Finding Andy 74
Only an idiot 84
A stable changed my life 95
Nikau reminder 105
The reluctant traveller 115
Cloud Farm is born 125
Solar power comes to Cloud Farm 133
Those last crucial steps 140
Making the break 149
Heather arrives 158
The garden tour 169
Epilogue 177
Historical note 180

I dedicate this book to my late parents,
Jean and Chris Chetwynd, for their constancy,
warmth and enjoyment of life.

You must be mad . . .

I was trying to delay my arrival and my boss's inevitable hearty welcome. As I walked down the familiar corridor I had to pass under the portraits of previous deans glaring down from their lofty heights. They looked more disapproving than ever. I avoided the recently purchased, politically correct piece of modern art which seemed more a barricade than a thing of beauty, and I negotiated the secretary's polite but possibly barbed enquires. Too soon, I was sitting in a comfortable chair with a coffee perched on my knees and the usual pleasantries dispatched. There was nothing for it but to tell him why I'd come.

His eyes were first to react, jerking open sharply to let me see inside the real person, just for a moment. This was a rare privilege for he was the model manager and nothing made him lose his cool; he had a smooth, studied solution for every problem. I suppose I could have felt complimented that my news had thrown him so off balance. Then he laughed — not uproariously — but rather shakily, another unexpected response and not a very professional one. Finally he found his tongue and asked a few probing questions, but he didn't seem to listen to my replies. He sympathised briefly about how demanding our jobs had become and confided how he frequently worked until three in the morning and how much his wife complained. Then something pulled him back to the present and he resumed his usual manner. Surely I didn't want to throw away my career at the medical school to go and live in the bush? Perhaps I was suffering from stress; maybe I should take a break from work and reconsider my decision?

An important call came through for him; our meeting finished abruptly, and I left his office feeling quite deflated. I had expected congratulations, even accolades for being so brave as to retire at 50 and start doing something completely different. As I walked back to my department I realised for the first time how strange my decision might appear to others.

The formal retirement dinner with the other heads of department was held some time later. It was like attending my own funeral. Men in grey suits said warm and almost witty things, sparring with each other to be seen as my closest friend. There were presents instead of wreaths, smiles instead of tears, but the atmosphere had the same air of loss that accompanies an unexpected death. In past times these men might have stabbed me in the back and tried to grab my budget for their own, yet now that I was leaving they felt betrayed and shocked that I was voluntarily giving up the life we had all sacrificed so much to achieve. None would miss me personally, none had been close to me, but my leaving upset their sense of equilibrium and belief in the value of the lives they were leading. It was only three years since I'd been made a professor and head of my department; in their terms I'd just reached the pinnacle of success. Now I was throwing it all away, not for an important job overseas, nor even for a better paid one in the north, but simply giving it up and going to live in an isolated part of the country. It was slightly crazy and unsettling. They wanted to get the funeral over with and return to the security of their offices and over-burdened schedules.

Now, some years on, I wonder where I got the strength to do it and whether I was a little bit crazy. At the time I was living alone, had very little money and practically no knowledge of farming or country life. Yet I felt determined to give up work and leave the city, throwing away all the privileges of a well-paid job to live in a small cottage on a mountainous piece of bush beyond the reaches of power lines or telephone poles. I had no idea what was the driving force behind all this but it gave me a sense of purpose and direction which brooked no second thoughts, questioning or doubts. I'm not normally an illogical or intuitive person given to flights of fancy or spontaneous decision-making. Rather, I am cautious, rational and patient. So how did I allow this other persona to take control of my life?

Dreaming of escape

It began harmlessly enough. I'd worked at the Christchurch School of Medicine for about 15 years and over that time the job had grown steadily until it dominated my life and thinking. Nothing particularly unusual in that — many jobs are worse — but with more and more of my days and nights absorbed by work I felt I was losing my sense of self.

I wasn't unhappy in my job — in many ways I loved it. I was lecturing and doing research in the medical discipline known as Public Health, my specialities being economics and health behaviour. I studied how people can prevent illness or improve their health and so reduce the need for medical care. I worked in a number of areas but when the AIDS epidemic broke out in the late 1980s it became my main interest, as I focussed on ways to prevent infection with the virus. This meant working with a wide variety of people. I was committed to what we were doing and fascinated by the challenges we faced. Along with this research and related policy work, I was on a few committees that give out grants for health research — a job that kept me in touch with developments in public health around the country.

But all this meant a huge amount of travelling and very little time for myself. At least once a week I'd fly to another part of the country where I saw nothing but the inside of a taxi and the sterile walls of a conference room. In winter I left home before dawn, returning after dark and wondering what the day had been like in my garden. But in summer, from the plane's tiny portholes, I caught tantalising views of the bush and the open country. Then I felt like a prisoner being transported in a paddy wagon between jails, glimpsing the real world through little grilled windows. I saw the greens of the trees without smelling their dampness, skimmed the tops of mountains without ever breathing their air.

On weekends, when my mind was a bit freer, I began to feel restless and have yearnings to 'get away from it all'. At first these were easy to deal with. Since I had no children to worry about, my weekends were free. My partner John and I would get in the car and drive for an hour or so to a country restaurant where he could relax over a good lunch while I looked out longingly at the cows and the distant hills. John isn't a rural person but was happy to indulge me as long as he could enjoy an element of it as well. We'd take Vita, our Tibetan terrier, and after lunch find a shady stream to walk along or a bubbling river where Vita could retrieve sticks from the shallows. John might sit somewhere cool and read while I listened for the sounds of birds in the surrounding bush.

One year we holidayed in Queenstown where John discovered the best coffee places and revelled in the international buzz, while I got my fill of the Remarkables mountain range and Lake Wakatipu, walking with Vita for miles around the lake's edge. I took a jet boat ride to the upper reaches of the Dart River and found solace in the peace of the high country and the clear, cool air.

On another holiday, with a couple of friends I walked the Routeburn Track in the Southern Alps, crossing a mountain pass at five thousand feet. There were two guides who carried everything we might need so that even someone as unfit as I could manage. I marvelled at my ability to walk four days on end despite years of sedentary living and some lingering weaknesses from a bout of childhood polio; it seemed the altitude and isolation were all the stimuli I needed.

But these excursions into the backcountry did nothing to satisfy my yearnings. Rather, they inspired me with confidence and a desire to go further. They were like the first tastes of an addictive drug; they offered temporary fulfilment but left me wanting more. They led me on an unknown path that promised happiness and freedom.

About this time my relationship with John ended. I don't know whether my rural leanings were a symptom or a cause of the breakdown, but we parted without acrimony, though with considerable sadness. Twelve years of living together meant habits had to be broken and comforts given up that had long been taken for granted. It took me ages to recover and adjust to a new life, but when John moved away from Christchurch, after a year or so, it was easier. I began to be comfortable with my aloneness and even to enjoy it.

During this time of loss and grieving my country desires had been put on hold, but work pressure continued unabated and my need to escape grew stronger than ever. I guess it was a sign of my recovery that I started to have the fantasies. These began innocently enough during my normal Saturday morning coffee ritual at the local café. Here, with the help of the newspaper, I began imagining a different life — one a world away from my weekday round. The fantasies started with the 'Livestock' column where you could find advertised Irish wolfhounds, exotic poultry, donkeys — creatures I could almost have managed on my suburban quarter-acre section, so the dreams weren't too extreme. Then I became more ambitious — there were llamas, highland cattle and Clydesdales. As the animals got bigger so did my imaginings and they led me to the 'Lifestyle Block' column. Sometimes I'd be living on '10 acres with magnificent country home in North Canterbury', then it would be '20 hectares for olive grove development' or maybe a partnership in a vineyard proposal.

Gradually my thoughts escalated and one day I started reading the 'Farms for Sale' column — one I'd never even noticed before. I didn't see myself as a sheep farmer but I liked the idea of a house in the country where I could walk through endless paddocks and ride over rolling hills. In this column I found huge tracts of land for the same price as a tiny inner city townhouse or a lifestyle block on the outskirts. For the next several months I was content just to contemplate '350 hectares in Oamaru with historic homestead', '80 acres in Okuti Valley with bush, streams and good building site', '600 acres overlooking the Hurunui with shepherd's cottage and outbuildings'. The choices were numerous and the dreams boundless.

Then somehow, without my knowing quite when, there was a sea change in my head and these thoughts became not just fantasies, but serious plans. I found myself genuinely wanting to buy some land in the country. What I intended to do with it or what this feeling of need meant I didn't know, but I began scanning the paper with new intensity and a sense of purpose. I had no ideas of leaving work or making any other changes to my life, but I was developing the idea of regenerating bush. Maybe, half consciously, I thought that giving something to help the life of the land would justify devoting so much of my own life to work.

At the same time, that work grew even more demanding. After my boss was promoted I was appointed to his job as Professor and Head of Department which meant I managed the staff and students in the disciplines of Public Health and General Practice as well as keeping up with my lecturing and research work. They were a great team of people and I enjoyed my new leadership role even though it meant more meetings and more frustrating administrative tasks and, of course, gave me even less time for myself. But there was a positive side to it. The new position gave me more money and now I could afford a mortgage to help me realise my dreams. I knew by now I wasn't interested in a lifestyle block on the margins of the city — I wanted a decent chunk of land with some bush and a house.

Whenever I had a spare moment from work my thoughts would return to the 'Farms for Sale' column. Although there were magnificent places all over the South Island, I had to limit the choices so I narrowed my search down to the Banks Peninsula. Being only an hour or so from Christchurch it seemed a good location and it's stunningly beautiful. Much of the land around the city is flat whereas the peninsula is formed from the cones of two extinct volcanoes which rise steeply from the harbours of Akaroa and Lyttelton up to two thousand feet or more. It is rugged, some of it is bush-clad and although by the sea it has a high country feel.

I knew nothing about buying farmland, what to look for,

or the pitfalls, but I have some knowledgeable friends who offered to come along to check out the possibilities. Ironically, when I started looking in earnest, there seemed to be few places on the market. Brocheries Flat was the first I found — about 75 acres of wonderful alpine-type meadow above the Akaroa township. It had an old hay shed, its views were great and the setting stunning, but my advisers were cautious because there was no house and it would be difficult to get the rights to build one. I let this go and it soon sold. With another friend I looked at Cherry Farm on the edge of Akaroa. A big house on 10 acres, it was lovely but the land was surrounded by residential development and they were asking a high price.

Weeks and months passed but few prospects arose. I took a polytechnic course on 'Buying a Small Block' so that I'd know what questions to ask when the land came up, but nothing did. It was the good times of the 1990s so prices were rising and sellers holding back. Someone advised I write to one farmer asking if he would sell me a bit of land, but I had no reply. Getting desperate, I began to suspect only locals could find land on the peninsula so I thought of buying an old cottage in Akaroa to become a local myself. I pursued this for a time but the deal on the cottage fell through when the owner upped his price at the last minute. I was beginning to lose hope.

Then one weekend in *The Press* I saw, 'House on 165 acres on Banks Peninsula, $155,000'. Suspiciously few details were given but it was in my price league and I thought it worth following up. None of my advisers was free to look at it with me, so on the Sunday I went alone. It was a dry warmish day in October, 1994. Spring was definitely on its way and I relished the drive to Akaroa. The harbour sparkled below as I crested the Hilltop and made my way around the bays to the township.

Buoyed by the excitement of the search I marched into the real estate office with the confidence of a city sophisticate. A large round man with a freshly scrubbed face greeted my enquiries with the usual smiles and politeness of his profession. He gave me the details of the property and showed me photos of the land and the map of its location. Explaining the state of its fences and the viability of its tracks, he speculated also on the reliability of the water supply and the average annual rainfall. When he asked what my plans for the farm would be I mumbled something uncertainly and tried to look knowing as he pointed out its boundaries and associated roads and landmarks. I didn't know where these were nor did I understand what he meant by a 'paper' road, but I wasn't used to being ignorant or out of my depth so I pretended otherwise. Finally he gave me the address, told me to go and have a look at the land and suggested we meet at a nearby road junction later so he could show me round the house.

I left his office much more tentatively than I'd entered it. The knowledge gained on my brief polytechnic course was beginning to wear thin and I hadn't even looked at the land yet. I retreated to the security of a café and boosted myself with a strong coffee. When I felt a bit calmer I set out.

For ten minutes I ground straight up the hill behind the Akaroa township. The steep and winding road was a challenge for any car, but I was relieved when mine, an elderly version of a European fashion statement, reached the summit. Here roads went off in all directions: down to the sea, left along the ridge, right through farmland, but an unprepossessing gravel road that led past an old quarry was the one I'd been told to take. Not far along, on the brow of the hill, I parked the car. The property was to my right and I wandered down the road looking across at the land, not very impressed. It was a steep hillside with scraggly shrubs dotting the paddocks. In the distance was a line of wind-battered old pines, presumably sheltering the house. A deep gully ran down the middle of the property and near the bottom I could see a man moving cattle. When he yelled at his dogs his voice carried up clearly in this natural amphitheatre. The cows' complaining moos and the dogs' urgent barks broke the otherwise total silence of the valley. Parked by the gate into the property was an ancient Landrover which I passed as I continued walking down the road. The silence grew. As I watched, the man took the cattle lower and lower into the valley, their sounds dying away as they went. No cars came down the road. No civilisation was apparent. I could have been the only one left on the planet. Even the birds seemed silent. Was this peace or was it eerie?

Then suddenly over the horizon came a yellow Honda. It parked perkily by the farm gate and a young couple got out, opened the back to put on gumboots and made their way cautiously down the farm track towards the house. They were obviously inspecting it with a view to purchase. A sense of repulsion and urgency rushed through me. Yellow ants from the town were invading this land. It deserved better.

In retrospect, I can see this was a pivotal moment. At this point I wasn't particularly taken with what I'd seen of the farm. I was almost scared by its air of desolation and the dramatic drive required to get to it. Yet when I saw these 'townies' treading its paths with their mincing steps and broaching its inner sanctum with unseemly haste, I felt a sense of maternal protectiveness such as you might have for a daughter who has become ensnared in a religious group. I knew I must prevent this land from falling into the 'wrong' hands. Why I should have been so arrogant as to think my hands were the 'right' ones I have no idea. But confidence can be a blinding thing.

I left the yellow ants to their inspection and went back up the road. The real estate man had told me to climb to the top of the ridge there and look down over the property to see the extent of remaining native bush. I scrambled straight up for about a hundred metres. From here I could look over the Akaroa Harbour in one direction, straight out across the Pacific Ocean in another and down the valley to a magnificent stand of native trees, so luxuriant and lush it looked almost like West Coast bush. Clouds raced above my head, mountain tussocks rustled in the wind, the air was fresh and clear. Far to the west I could see the Alps. Under my feet mosses and orchids competed for hold on the rocky surface.

I'd had little time to take it all in before I saw the agent arrive at our meeting spot. I began to make my way back to the road. The slope was almost vertical, the surface uneven and there was no path. I'd clambered up with the agility of a mountain goat, but getting down was painfully slow as I tried to protect a once-dislocated knee and once-broken ankle, both of which were objecting to this sudden trauma. My shortened Achilles tendon, a legacy of the polio, made my gait more awkward than ever on this steep surface. I could see the man watching from his car and remembered his comfortable solidity and sturdy legs. He would have had no difficulty negotiating the hill. I felt exposed as a fraud, trying to portray myself as knowledgeable and confident in the country, yet struggling to get down a simple hillside. I imagined what he must be thinking as I finally arrived at his car.

Revealing none of his doubts, he was charming and informative as we drove to the house. At the gate I was pleased to see the yellow Honda had gone — I wasn't in the mood for polite conversation with competitors. We turned onto the farm track with some difficulty but the agent assured me it was basically sound though suitable only for four-wheel drives in winter. Halfway along he pointed out the spring which he thought could provide a year-round water supply.

Beside the farmhouse a line of tall, battered macrocarpas provided shelter from what, judging by their shape, must have been a fierce prevailing wind. Parking as close as possible, we made our way down a steep hillside for a hundred metres or so to the back door of a small square wooden structure with a rusting roof. Here the agent's selling techniques began to fail him. The door swung open to disclose silver paper-clad walls, a stench of rats and their droppings, a missing window pane where rain had come in, and a hole in the ceiling with corresponding hole in the floor created by decades of drips. A piece of corrugated iron hung where there should have been a front door. There was an old crumbling fireplace and a disgusting kitchen unit, now a mortuary for moths, flies and spiders.

I think the agent murmured something about sound construction and solid totara but he was strangely mute as I looked into each of the hideous bedrooms where junk enough for a dozen garage sales had accumulated over the years. Crude bunk beds straddled one of the rooms, and mattresses, home to a million dust mites, lay haphazardly around. The whole place was dark and dirty, there was no water, power, or bathroom. The agent pointed to a hut under a tree in the distance and said that would be the long-drop toilet.

There was nothing much for either of us to say. I could almost feel the resignation in his stomach. He returned me to my car and we parted with the usual assurances of getting back in touch. I drove quietly back to the city, seeming quite unmoved, neither disgusted nor excited by what I'd seen, but I noticed that a sense of calm had descended over me like a soft blanket of mist.

That night I had dinner with two of my oldest friends. I told them about the farm in a matter-of-fact sort of way. 'It's got wonderful bush, it's got a house, it's in my price range and I'd get 165 acres for my money. What do you think?' One of them replied immediately, 'Oh I would go for it Jane'. We didn't discuss it much and the conversation soon moved on to something else.

The next morning it was back to work as usual. There was a meeting of heads of department to talk about timetabling for the coming year, an innocent-sounding, but crucial, battle ground in medical school politics where you had to ensure students got as much time as possible on your speciality — staff numbers and budgetary allocations depended on it. I couldn't afford to lose concentration or I might lose a staff member or two as well, so thoughts of the farm were put on hold. But at last the meeting was over and as soon as I was back in my office I rang the estate agent and made an offer. Hiding his surprise with a skill that reflected his years in the business, he agreed to pass the offer on to the owners.

I felt serene and sure, as though I knew exactly what I was doing. I'd called my advisers to tell them and one, who'd long supported me on the farm-buying trail, went straight over to the peninsula and had a look. She came back horrified, saying it was a dreadful wind trap, freezing cold; there was driving sleet and the house was unimaginably disgusting. Her comments made no impact. I was not to be discouraged.

Next day the estate agent called me at work with a counter-offer. Suddenly the logical part of my brain recovered itself, swinging into action to make me start feeling anxious. If I accepted, the farm was mine, which meant real commitment — much more scary than merely putting in an offer. I went home at lunchtime and rang a friend who calmed my fears, saying I should go with my feelings. Calling the agent back, I accepted.

Another adviser went over to look at the farm and came back ecstatic, saying it was paradise: the sun shone, the birds sang, the site was magnificent, and the bush stunning.

My offer was conditional for a couple of weeks so I could still get out of it if I had to. I asked some friends who farmed near the property to give me an opinion, and arranged to meet them there the following Saturday. I parked on the road and walked down the farm track into slanting needles of rain which bit into my face. The howl of the wind would have made it impossible to talk. I got there first so went to the house to wait, managing to open the rusty old padlock on the back door so I could shelter inside. Soon I saw the others making their way slowly along the track. Even they, real farmers, had parked at the gate rather than brave the track with their vehicle.

We yelled at each other through the gale as I stumbled up to meet them. Inspecting the possible water supply, they said the spring just needed a bit of clearing up since the cattle had made it all puggy. However, they suggested the weather might be a bit of a problem, mentioning low cloud and sea mist which hung around at this height, and snow which could cut off the property for a fortnight or more in winter. I answered them with a shrug of my rain-coated shoulders, telling them I loved weather like that — it was just right for someone born in the far north of England.

When we got inside the house they laughed, saying it was much the same as one of the old cottages on their property and then, looking vainly around for something positive to remark on, said how fortunate it hadn't been vandalised. They were encouraging, saying they'd like to have me as a neighbour, offering to help with bulldozing a track and volunteering their son to clean up the spring. Apparently they told each other in private that it wasn't a property for a woman on her own, but they said nothing of this to me. I think they sensed my resolve.

Life at work went on regardless of these farming distractions and I had to go off to England for a conference on health economics. The legal papers for the purchase of the farm came through by fax to the University of York. The conference secretary handed them to me just as I was going into a workshop on the economic impact of AIDS. It was all a bit surreal. I escaped at the tea break and sat in a strange office overlooking a neat, ordered landscape and considered the various deeds and documents. There were one or two complications but nothing serious, my lawyer advising that I could go ahead. I faxed my signed copy. I'd had little experience of buying property but faxes did make it easier and less formal. I thought back to my first house purchase when John and I had had to provide the bank manager with reams of evidence of our finances. Now the banks seemed to be throwing money away — there were no obstacles in the way of my purchasing a farm despite my complete lack of experience.

On the 1st of December, two weeks after my return to New Zealand, the farm would be mine.

When dreams come to land

At 4 p.m. that day the lawyer rang me at work back in Christchurch to say it had all gone through. Sounding almost as excited as I was, he overcame his normal reserve to make a wisecrack about landed gentry. I can't remember whether I managed a suitable reply but I know I went home in a daze, gliding along familiar routes on autopilot then almost forgetting where I'd stored the celebratory bottle of wine. As a child I'd always wanted to be a farmer's wife and now, forty years on, here I was, a farmer. Toasting my own good fortune, I looked out the windows at my spruce suburban garden. I imagined wild rolling hills and sweeping landscapes as I'd done so often before, but this time the dreams had substance.

I'd taken only a couple of sips of wine and had very few minutes to savour my new status when the phone rang: the 'noxious weeds' officer from the Regional Council wanted to discuss the control of gorse on my farm. Sounding serious and sombre, he outlined my legal responsibilities and emphasised the importance of eradicating this weed. I had only a vague notion of what gorse was, some sort of shrub with yellow flowers, and I wasn't in the mood for a lecture, so I cut him off with the briskness bred of years dealing with telemarketers. Now I can see his call as an omen of things to come but at that moment, with the euphoria of the purchase and the mellow taste of the wine, I felt no concern.

The next day was a Friday so I took it off from work, packing a picnic and my dog Vita into the car to go over to the farm. Being head of department had some advantages when it came to wagging work! I arrived about midday and strode through the gate knowing that I was on my own land for the first time. As I walked down towards the house my excitement began to mount. The main valley looked completely different: the scrubby shrubs I had seen in early spring were now green and glorious fuchsia, one of the few deciduous native trees, and the paddocks were covered with them. On my first visit I'd thought this gully unimpressive, almost dreary. Now it was lush, dramatic and endlessly inviting.

Leaving our few provisions at the house, Vita and I began to explore the main track which meandered gently downhill. Below us the sea was a constant presence, stretching out to meet the sky along a blurry horizon. Distant headlands were etched with the outlines of boulders and wind-blown trees while on nearby hills sheep slowly munched their way around the contours. Hebes and five-fingers lined our way, intermingled with ferns and pepper trees. Every now and then the track crossed a stream where the water had carved out a runway and left a legacy of thick, green growth. Jumping and splashing across, I tried not to wet my socks so early in the day. Halfway down the track we came to a fence line and closed gate which could have been the boundary, but we carried on through it, gambling that we were still on 'my land' which just seemed to go on and on with different and wonderful views around every bend. It felt remote and safe, desolate yet peaceful.

After an hour or so on the track, I made my way back up to the house for lunch, this time taking the more direct route straight up the bank. It was well past noon and I'd thought I was hungry but once inside the house, I couldn't bear to eat, or even to take the lid off the thermos flask; the rat smell and dirt were overwhelming! So I found an abandoned stool and had my first meal sitting outside the front door or, to be more precise, by the corrugated iron-covered hole where it used to be, and gazed out at the bay below.

It was a dull day with low cloud but nothing could dampen my enthusiasm. Slowly, almost ceremoniously, I ate my sandwiches, feeling satisfied with my purchase. The land and its tracks were far more enticing than I'd remembered and even the house, despite its squalor, was beginning to show me its charm. It had been a very humble dwelling, square in shape with a corridor running down its centre and divided into four identically sized rooms. From the front it looked entirely symmetrical: an entrance doorway flanked by two large windows. The roof was high and steep with an old chimney pot its crowning feature. I could imagine that when it had been young and well cared for, the house would have looked like a child's painting with smoke drifting from its chimney and curtains softening its windows. Even its location on the land seemed comfortable. The house nestled into the hillside on a small shelf of rock, while at the front where the land dropped steeply away, its face was set firmly to the sea. Bush provided shelter from the south, while the line of old macrocarpas protected the other side.

Sitting on my stool I began to feel an almost spiritual calm of the sort I'd experienced only once or twice before at places of ancient religious significance, like the ruined Riveaulx Abbey in Yorkshire. There was something harmonious in the lie of the land that produced a deep sense of well-being. Only Vita, begging for the last of the sandwiches, brought me back to reality. Perhaps I was reading too much into the feelings on my first day, or perhaps the rat smell was affecting my mind. I got resolutely to my feet; it was time to walk the top boundary.

Behind the house, I made my way up through the paddocks to the highest peak on the ridge-line. There I looked down again over the bush-clad gully I had viewed that first day. It was like a rain forest, dense with vegetation in hundreds of shades of green and brown that blended softly to the eye. Only the grey bark of dead trunks stood out against the wall of colour and the occasional frond of a tree fern broke its outline. I stood for some time trying to take in the beauty of the scene while inside me excitement and serenity contended.

But I'd come up to inspect the boundaries so I pushed onwards along the ridge and down to the fence-line which I began to follow back. Adopting what I thought was a professional manner, I checked out the wiring, noting an occasional post which needed replacing. My neighbour's woolly sheep on the other side looked harmless enough but I didn't want them getting through into 'my' bush with their voracious appetites. In only 24 hours I had become zealously protective of this land.

I was concentrating so hard on the fence that I didn't notice the change in the weather but suddenly, from nowhere, cloud came down and I was enveloped in thick fog. This was the sea fret my farming friends had warned me about, but it was denser and more frightening than I'd imagined. There was total silence. Birds stopped singing as if night had fallen and any other sound was immediately muffled. I was disoriented with the loss of sight and sound; I could see nothing beyond about ten metres. I knew roughly where I was but began to doubt myself in this strange landscape and almost lost my bearings simply following the fence-line. Vita stayed close beside me as we made our way back to familiar territory and finally to the house.

With the view obliterated I had little desire to stay. Packing up, I went down to the safety and familiarity of Akaroa where I bought myself a large serving of fish and chips to take back to a friend's empty holiday house in the neighbouring valley. The meal was exquisite, and there was real joy in making a cup of tea, turning on the radio and going to the inside toilet. I began to appreciate that civilization had a lot going for it!

After a good sleep, I woke to see 'my property' out through the kitchen window then spent the morning walking more of the land, learning to identify its boundaries. The agent had shown me them on a map but I've never been good at converting such images into hills and gullies so I was slow to realise the full extent of the farm. There was a lot more land than I'd appreciated and because it was so steep, the acreage was much greater than if it were on the flat.

The deep strip of bush to the south of the house was alluring but seemed inaccessible. A break in the fence near the farm track suggested a path should start there, but it was steep, with fallen branches and bush lawyer blocking any way in. Scrabbling along the bush edge I found at last the outline of a rough path immediately behind the house. A short way along this, hidden discretely around a bend, was a pile of old boards, one featuring a large round hole. The original earth toilet's contents had long since returned to nature and the skeletal remains of the shed were covered with moss. Beyond, the path carried on through the bush. It wound past huge totaras and broadleafs whose height I could only guess at as they shot skywards. Underneath were ferns, hanging off branches, poking through holes in rocks, covering old stumps. And there were the fuchsias. Here in the bush they were not just shrubs but large old trees, their pink trunks twisted and turned, reflecting years of struggle for a share of the light.

As I went deeper into the bush a pair of fantails accompanied my every step, darting about after the insects I disturbed, while overhead, the song of bellbirds punctured the silence. This was original forest dating back well before European settlement — its trees had seen generations of people, its soil had lain untouched for centuries. I felt as if I had walked into my own national park. This bush had looked wonderful from above, but to be in amongst it, a part of it and cosseted by it — these were delights I had not even imagined. The path gradually narrowed and came to an end in a thicket of creepers which seemed impenetrable. Leaving any further exploring for another day I set off back to the house and felt the warmth of the sun as I emerged from the cool green of the undergrowth.

By now it was bright and clear so I took my sandwiches up to the paddock above the house to eat lunch with a different view of the ocean. From here the horizon between sky and sea was split by a broad headland that separated the wide expanse of one sandy bay from the winding river-fed valley of another. Far out at sea a container ship drifted towards South

America but there was no other sign of human life, no rumble of traffic, no cell phone towers, no jets overhead. How had I stumbled into such paradise? The pervasive quiet seemed enfolding, not frightening; time had no importance, but the land was all.

The sound of an engine broke my reveries and over the hill came Dee, my first visitor. As her ugly black van made its way down my drive for the first time I found myself eager to share all my excitements and discoveries. Dee had been a strong supporter in my search for land and she'd also been an inspiration in my personal journey to this point. She was a psychiatric nurse by day while at home on the farm she and her partner bred horses and kept a few sheep. To see them running such a venture in their spare time had helped me realise that I could do something similar. It was almost two years to the day since my first visit to her farm; now here I was welcoming her to mine.

With our three dogs in tow, Dee and I made our way to the highest point of the property to view its full extent. I had become familiar with the pattern of distant fence-lines and how they translated into my land versus another's, so I felt rather knowledgeable as I pointed out my boundaries, without letting on about my earlier ignorance. We scrambled down a gully I hadn't yet explored, passing through waist-high gorse and bracken and discovering a spring on the way. My recent polytech course had instilled in me the importance of water so I felt smug about this little hidden asset, as if I'd found a jewel in the attic of my new house. I doubted this spring would have any practical use — I wasn't going to have animals on the property — but there is something magical about water bubbling directly out of a rocky hillside.

We got back to the house in time to welcome more friends who arrived bearing champagne which it seemed proper to open on the highest point, so after a brief tour of the house, we made our way back up to the ridge-line to sit looking over the ocean and bush as we drank to my new venture. The sun was obligingly bright, the wind dropped to a gentle breeze and the water sparkled below us. Everyone seemed delighted by the land and its views but even the effects of the alcohol couldn't endear the house to them. Although they didn't say much I knew it horrified them and that they doubted I could ever make it habitable, but I didn't care; their general encouragement and warmth were all I needed.

That champagne was the first of many I've consumed on the ridge top, and although the bubbles then were particularly sparkling, they have been just as satisfying ever since. That spot, with its views in all directions, remains my favourite place for a celebration. Whether I'm toasting birthdays, babies, books being published, or just the sunset at the end of another day, it's always hard to tear myself away and it's usually only approaching darkness or storms that force me to leave.

But that day we had an appointment so after the alcohol had settled we left the farm and went over to Hinewai, the property on my southern boundary, where I was to meet the manager, Hugh Wilson. A highly regarded botanist and conservationist, Hugh was known to me by reputation. I had admired him for some time; he ran the largest private nature reserve on the peninsula. The four of us drove to the car park and walked down half a kilometre or more of fairly steep track to his house. Hugh had banned all cars from the reserve which meant everyone had to walk in. That is not too arduous for day visitors, but Hugh had to haul all his supplies and materials down this track either on his back or in the panniers of his pushbike. He was well known for his antipathy towards cars and went everywhere by bike, including to Christchurch 85 kilometers away.

I didn't know what to expect of this paragon of principle but I approached his house with some trepidation and found myself hanging back behind the others as we got nearer. Greetings in Maori erupted from somewhere in the garden and a small gnome-like figure rushed out to meet us. He was a combination of Father Christmas and Superman with his round rosy face framed by white hair and beard, and the kind of trim muscular body that a gym addict would die for. Energy exuded from every pore as he rushed about showing us special plants and organising tea for everyone, his conversation peppered with deep roars of laughter. But despite the bustle, there was a confidence and calm about him that reminded me of a Tibetan monk.

Hugh seemed pleased to have me as a neighbour and offered lots of help including a hand-drawn map of my property which he'd done a few years earlier, and a promise to visit me soon to discuss his methods of dealing with gorse, the so-called noxious weed. We left after a frenetic hour or so and I drove back to Christchurch thoroughly exhausted but cheered by everyone's encouragement.

Waking the next morning I felt heavy-headed and overwhelmed. Meeting Hugh had been a joy; he was enthusiastic, helpful and an expert in his field — what a stroke of luck to have him as my neighbour. On the other hand, his standards were so high and he was so dedicated and committed to the cause of conservation that I felt worried. Could I ever meet his expectations or would I disappoint him? Fortunately, it was Sunday and I didn't have to work. I lay in bed all morning drinking copious cups of tea and tried to take in all that I'd seen and heard in the two days I'd spent at the farm.

Hugh's map showed all the tracks on my land, including one through the bush, and it marked the significant areas of remnant and regenerating bush. He'd also given me a list of plants and tree species he'd found in a botanical survey of the property some years earlier, a good guide to what I could expect to grow in the future, but for now it was the map that gave me the most pleasure. I was still having some difficulty getting the geography of the land sorted out in my head but here, in Hugh's quaint script, was the whole farm laid out before me. Reminiscent of a map of Middle Earth from a Tolkien book, it was child-like in its simplicity but carried the promise of adventure and escapade. Now I had a clear picture of fence-lines and boundaries, of forests and tracks and, as if a fog had lifted, I could see the whole property for the first time.

I spent that afternoon as I usually did on weekends: having late and leisurely brunch with friends, visiting an art gallery or two, then walking in the Botanical Gardens. Somehow, though, the distractions didn't have their usual appeal. Normally on Sundays I felt tired and lazy, capable of nothing more than quietly absorbing culture or food or conversation, but today I was full of energy, too excited to be a properly laid-back city dweller. I was unsatisfied and bored by this kind of passivity.

Looking back I can see this as the first sign that the farm was beginning to change me. I'd owned it for only three days but already it was beginning to erode my sense of fulfilment in the city. Later it would begin to make me doubt my sense of worth at work too, but for now it was merely giving me a brief glimpse into the futility of the life I'd been leading.

The day of the bonfires

In mid-December Christchurch begins its Christmas celebrations with a Saturday night performance of Handel's *Messiah* at the Town Hall. This year I'd made my arrangements well in advance to be sure of good company and seats. As usual, the concert was magnificent but as I tried to settle into the music and join the audience in hushed attention, I found it hard to bring my mind back from the farm where I'd spent the day.

The goal had been to clear out the house, something I couldn't possibly have managed on my own with the stench of rats and mounds of insect carcasses but my friend Dee was undaunted by the task, adamant that we'd have it clean in no time. She told me I'd never make a farmer if I couldn't handle a bit of rat poo — it was more like a tsunami of rat poo to me — so I willingly accepted her help.

We drove over to the farm early and began by dragging everything outside — old mattresses, half-eaten cardboard boxes, rusty paint tins, broken chairs, filthy blankets — decades of accumulated discards. It was a dreary task made more so when it began to drizzle, but then Dee suggested we start a bonfire to burn some of the junk. Ten years living in Australia had made me cautious about outside fires but such reticence was soon overcome by the warmth of the blaze and satisfaction at getting rid of the rubbish. As the rain increased so did the size of the fire until we'd cleared all but the front room. I could never have done this without Dee's help, my dislike of handling filthy and dusty things being almost pathological, but I got no sympathy from her; apparently working as a psychiatric nurse had cured her of any scruples about dirt!

We took a quick break and went down to Akaroa for lunch and a good wash in the public toilets — my first visit to the facilities with which I was to become very familiar. Since I had neither running water nor a toilet at the farm, my appreciation for the public facilities grew with every visit, as it did for the village of Akaroa with all it had to offer. Set in its peaceful and gently curving bay, it was a great antidote to the rugged and comfortless atmosphere of the farmhouse. Although it has few permanent residents, Akaroa serves a big tourist market, so its cafés, restaurants and winebars match the best in the country. Only ten minutes' drive from the farm, it was to become my sanctuary in the coming months, providing hygiene and luxury when the dereliction and dirt of the old house got too much.

That day we lunched on huge bowls of seafood chowder sitting by an open fire with Mozart in the background lulling us into a false sense of languor. It was hard to return to an afternoon of drudgery on a windswept mountainside, particularly as the weather had now deteriorated from foggy drizzle to full-blown rain. But once back there I got an even larger rubbish fire going while Dee dragged out all the old timber and rat-nibbled cartons from the front room. Whatever seemed worth keeping we stored in the back shed, everything else was tossed on the fire. It was addictive, seeing how quickly the fire consumed the junk. By the end of the day we had the house clear of all but the largest pieces. There were still some old chairs and chests of drawers lying about but Dee persuaded me that these might be useful in the future and should be spared the fire.

To reward ourselves for all this hard work, we set off for a walk down the farm track and the rain conveniently stopped. We marvelled at the regenerating bush while the dogs rushed about discovering possum smells at every turn. Too soon it was time to head back to the city so after loading the van with unburnable rubbish, we laid down rat poison and sped home. Dee dropped me off minutes before I had to set out again for the concert.

In the auditorium my friends sat on one side of me while on the other was a woman in a wonderful cream silk outfit. It must have been brand new because every fold and pleat was immaculate, every seam where it should be. She exuded correctness, cleanliness and corsets, her perfume reminding me of a duty-free shop in some exotic location. I looked down at my hands; the quick shower hadn't been enough to dislodge all the evidence of my day's activities. Discreetly I placed them in the pockets of my jacket. The woman caught my eye and smiled warmly as one music lover to another, not noticing anything untoward. But I felt a bit guilty and a little conspiratorial; would she be quite so relaxed if she knew that only hours before I'd been up to my elbows in rat droppings and dead flies? I was beginning to live a double life — and to enjoy it. Grinning inwardly, I leaned back and stretched out my tired legs, hoping her expensive perfume would overpower the eau de bonfire emanating from the bits of me that had escaped the hurried shower.

I remember feeling cross with myself during the concert for being unable to switch off from the farm and focus on the music but, in retrospect, I can see that this was expecting a lot. I was still in a state of great excitement over my new purchase and that day, the day of the bonfires, marked the beginning of its transformation.

It wasn't only in social situations that I was having trouble concentrating. It was hard at work too. With only a couple of weeks to go before the Christmas break, things were slowing down — exams were over, marking was finished and the students had gone off for their summer holidays. Every day I went in to the medical school as usual and went through the motions of working, but during dreary meetings or when I was alone in the office I'd often find my thoughts turning to farm matters and the challenges they presented.

Most pressing of these was to get some heating into the house and I fancied an old coal range of the type that would have been in the house originally. In my childhood in Northumberland we'd heated a huge old rectory with an Aga — a coal-burning stove which never went out. With this we did all the cooking and baking, heated the hot water, dried the washing and kept the kitchen as warm as a womb despite its flagstone floor and large windows.

This was the image I had in my mind as I began the search for a stove. I enlisted the help of my friend Sue, a West Coaster and consequently an expert on coal ranges, and together we searched the largest demolition yards in Christchurch. We found a couple of rather shabby, unimpressive ones before we got lucky. Away in a far corner of one yard, but shining like the dawn sun rising from the sea, was a bright red range with a large surround. Not only beautiful, it was also in very good condition, but the question was, would it fit in the fireplace? Sue offered to come out with me the following day to measure up and I made arrangements to take the day off work.

It was a warm, cloudless and windless morning. As I drove up the last ridge before the farm, Sue became ecstatic about the shape of the hills, the beauty of the boulders and the softness of the tussock against the solid volcanic rock. She is an artist and all these were joy to a painter's heart. I'd been a bit nervous about whether she would like the property but when we finally crested the hill and saw the ocean sparkling before us, with the house tucked away behind the trees, she was delighted. She demanded I stop the car and jumped out to see the full view. Once the engine had died the silence was overwhelming and then as our ears attuned, the birdsong became clear: an underlay of intimate murmurings from the smaller birds, pierced by the more insistent calls and cries of bellbirds.

We made our way slowly down the bank to the house and with some pride I undid the padlock on the back door. Since our marathon efforts at clearing out the rubbish, the house was beginning to look more habitable and feel less like a wildlife reserve, but I was forgetting that Sue hadn't seen its former state. To her it appeared totally derelict, issuing a challenge beyond anything she'd imagined. For a moment her usual optimism was stalled. But she soon recovered and entered into the spirit of renovation, spending several hours contemplating how to get warmth, light and life back into the place.

We measured up the fireplace and found that it was too small for the beautiful coal range though Sue said the chimney-breast could be altered to fit. We threw around ideas of this sort for some time before she came up with a more radical suggestion: why not abandon the romantic notion of a coal range and put in an efficient log-burner which would heat the house and the water? I could use gas for cooking.

When we got back to Christchurch my head was buzzing and I spent the rest of the week mentally redesigning the house. I realised the restoration was going to be quite a challenge — not daunting, but exciting, and well beyond anything I'd done before. I needed some professional help and was recommended a local architect who arranged to meet me at the farm the next Saturday, as did a local builder who would advise me on whether the chimney, with its crumbling mortar, was safe to use. So far I'd resisted lighting a fire in case the chimney caught alight and burnt the house down.

That weekend I planned to spend my first night at the farm and Dee offered to support me in this brave undertaking so I picked her up after work on Friday, getting out there about 7.30 p.m. We heated up baked beans on a camping stove and as it was a perfect clear night sat outside looking down over the bay as the light faded. I had now owned the farm for two weeks and my first real test of loyalty was coming up. As darkness fell I wondered, could I possibly sleep in this rat-infested, dirty, draughty house?

In the back bedroom were two old bunks made of rusty wires stretched from one wall to the other and on these we placed various rugs, paddings and sleeping bags. As darkness grew there was nothing for it but to go to bed, arranging the three dogs around the floor to sleep on their own blankets and, hopefully, to keep the rats away. Clambering into the bunks, we bravely blew out the candles. The pitch black was omnipresent and claustrophobic; even after my eyes adjusted I could see nothing inside or out of the window.

I don't believe I slept at all. Every time a dog moved or sighed in its sleep I thought it was a rat and whenever a board creaked or a window shook I thought it was a rat. And once the wind got up there was plenty of shaking and creaking to occupy the mind. The wind also brought the temperature down — the cold grew pervasive and relentless as draughts came through the floorboards and icy chills seeped through the bare glass of the windows. I had never been so uncomfortable as I was then, huddled shivering and anxious inside my sleeping bag. Dee slept solidly, oblivious to it all, while I lay awake and alive to every sound. Once I heard the scuttling of rats' feet in the roof but there was no other sign of life. Around dawn, as the first touches of light began to appear, I fell asleep, at last able to give up my vigil and let the light and the dogs protect me.

After such a miserable night I needed some luxury to restore my spirits so we drove over the hill and down to Akaroa where we had huge café lattes and even larger chocolate-filled croissants. This area had been settled by the French in the 1800s and that morning I was very grateful to those who had kept their traditions alive, and even more grateful to those who had Kiwi-ised them so that the portions were enough to feed 'real men'.

With stomachs full and caffeine-induced highs we returned to the farm to meet the architect. An urbane, silver-haired, smooth-skinned gentleman parked his stylish car at the farm gate and walked purposefully down the track to the house.

He looked a bit out of place picking his way over the holes in the floor and avoiding the worst excesses of dust and spiders' webs as he peered into roof cavities. But he assured me he'd been brought up on a farm and knew the smells of sheep dung and the problems of wind in exposed places. He said the first job should be re-piling, that if I didn't straighten out the foundations there was a chance any other improvement I made, like roofing or cladding, would twist out of shape in time and be wasted. I liked him — he was enthusiastic without being unrealistic and left promising a redesign that kept the character of the place without my spending too much money.

As he drove away, the builder arrived, and spent very little time in the roof space before concluding that the chimney was unsafe to use. The mortar was so old it was falling away from the bricks. He recommended pulling the chimney down and rebuilding from scratch; there were already signs of scarring on the wooden roof beams where sparks and flames had made their way through gaps in the bricks.

I was strangely relieved to have this opinion as it confirmed my fears about lighting a fire in the house and freed me from using the existing structure. I was able to think more laterally now about future layout.

As soon as the builder left, Dee and I returned to Christchurch for a party where again I felt a bit dislocated, conscious of my contrasting selves. Only hours before, I'd been sleeping, or trying to, in a rat-infested hovel, but now I was sipping wine and nibbling on feta-stuffed olives amongst clean and shining people. The paths of my public and private lives were beginning to diverge. To the outside world I was running a university department and taken up with all the worries of failing students and academic politics. I was expected to be interested in the applicants for the Chair in Surgery or in the pass rate of our students compared to that of Dunedin's. Rather, I was preoccupied with questions of how to get my farm-house heated, weatherproofed and secure, what to do with my land and how to control the weeds.

I slept well that night in my own warm and comfortable bed and woke full of plans to reorganise the farmhouse. If I took out the fireplace and the remainder of the wall dividing the kitchen and front room, I would have a large living area in which to put a free-standing log-burner for heating house and water. Suddenly this seemed such an obvious way to proceed: it was like a fog lifting and the path becoming so clear you wonder why you've never seen it before. This whole venture was becoming a lesson in trust: trust in my inner feelings and in going with them; trust that the solution would come; trust that the Universe would provide.

A couple of days later this lesson was underscored. I'd bought the farm with an almost 100 per cent mortgage, knowing that I could afford the repayments in the short term but that it would leave me little money for renovation. Some years before, I'd bought a small house in England — it had been important for my sense of security and belonging after my parents' deaths, but I had long since decided to sell it and completely pull up my English roots. Unfortunately the property market in that part of the country was depressed with nothing selling so I'd taken it off the market and lent it to a friend. Then, out of the blue, during my visit back there in November, it had sold privately and now the money came through. I was able to pay off a large chunk of the mortgage on the farm and leave myself a bit of cash to do up the house and maybe do some planting. It seemed like a lot of money to me and I was optimistic that it would go a long way but, in the years to come, I was to discover that farms eat dollars as if they are fertiliser pellets and only rarely do they give any back.

A different way of looking at it

It was almost the end of the year and time to make my annual visit to the accountant to file a tax return. Tony is a thin man of indeterminate age who in appearance fits the stereotype of his profession, but there the comparisons end. He is surprisingly chatty, always keen to find out what's going on and to offer advice accordingly.

This day he was even more talkative than usual and I found myself telling him about the farm — cautiously, in case he'd think I'd been frivolous. I knew he wouldn't approve of illogical pursuits of fancy, particularly when they involved large mortgages. So the version of the story I told him wasn't quite the one I've told here. To him I gave the impression that I saw the farm as an investment, as a means to ensure compulsory saving of my recent salary increase, and as a holiday house. I didn't mention Saturday morning fantasies or yellow ants or feelings of spiritual fulfilment amongst the rat droppings.

Surprisingly, Tony greeted the news of my purchase with enthusiasm and went on to suggest I set it up as a GST-registered business which would allow me to claim back the tax on the purchase price and expenses. His reaction jolted me into a very different way of looking at the farm, since I'd never thought of it as a commercial exercise. Something clicked inside my head although at this stage it wasn't a conscious thought — more like a jigsaw piece finding its mate. I'd bought the farm as a fantasy, an escape from the realities of life in the workplace; until now I hadn't considered it as an alternative to the workplace.

That night one of the local farmers rang to ask if he could rent some of my land for grazing his cattle. Apparently there'd been a drought and they were very short of feed. I was torn between wanting to help him out and not wanting any of the bush eaten. Reluctantly, I turned him down, but he seemed friendly and took my refusal well. A couple of days later another neighbour rang with the same request. I don't know how either of these men found out my name or telephone number, but it brought home to me that they were serious and concerned about their livelihoods. It helped me realize that the farm was an important resource and I must treat it accordingly, not just as a professional's plaything.

These requests and my accountant's attitude showed me what a responsibility it was to own a farm. Perhaps I'd been a bit irrational in buying it but I had to be businesslike in my approach to it now and although I'd owned the farm for only three weeks, the pressure was building to decide what to do with it. Previous owners had had plans approved for forestry and some planting had begun. Indeed, growing trees on this land made a lot of sense, but on the other hand I wanted to encourage the native bush to re-establish, so I had serious dilemmas. I wouldn't rush into decisions but the problems were beginning to become apparent. There was more to this than walking joyfully along tracks admiring the views with no responsibilities except to keep the gates shut.

In the final week before the Christmas break I took the Friday off work and went over to the farm. Driving up the last hill to the property I noticed large areas of pale, parched earth amongst the green and thought how dry it must be getting. Only as I got closer did I realise these pale patches were mounds of hailstones, lying like snowdrifts against the hill. There must have been a major storm the previous night and up here near the clouds the sun hadn't yet melted them. Vita was in doggy heaven, rolling and rolling until her long coat was heavy with balls of ice. The wild foxgloves shone out against their sparkling backdrop and I marvelled at the possibility of my first white Christmas in New Zealand. December was meant to be the beginning of summer but maybe on a farm two thousand feet high I could expect a different climate.

I wanted to get a better idea of the tree plantings so I set off down the farm track to the bottom paddocks, coming first to a gully of young gums, with leaves rattling in the breeze. Further down I found a large semicircle of radiata pines sheltering an area where several different species grew in clusters. Sadly these trees had been badly eaten by stock. Perhaps some would recover, but now they were just a pitiful collection of broken branches and bare stick-like trunks. In another paddock were Douglas firs like baby Christmas trees and larches reaching gracefully out to each other. Young Tasmanian blackwoods, also very badly chewed, showed signs of sending out new life while some oak-like trees were struggling to survive.

Finding all these trees was both exciting and depressing; it was exciting to discover this treasure-trove of potential, but depressing to know that someone had let stock do so much damage in such a short time. A fisherman by trade, the man who'd sold me the farm had owned it for only nine months but in that time his cattle had chewed and trampled their way through years of careful planting and nurturing by the previous owners. It was far too early to know how many of these trees would recover from their excessive pruning so early in life, but I was pleased with what remained. I made my way back to the house over a hillside dotted with stakes to which trees, or their remnants, were attached.

The next day was Christmas Eve and I headed into the mountains to spend the holiday with friends at Arthur's Pass and afterwards to camp on the West Coast for a few days. Worry about trees and such matters combined with uncomfortable sleeping conditions gave me several sleepless hours. Rain drove us home earlier than expected and my New Year's resolutions for 1995 were all about farming and getting on top of my decisions. The joy of owning land in the country was beginning to be coloured by the strain of its responsibilities.

Fortunately the summer break from the medical school gave me a chance to get some order back into my life. In the brief time since I'd bought the farm my head had been bombarded with ideas, excitements, possibilities and problems and I needed to get some structure into these thoughts before they took me over. Also, when the term started in a couple of weeks, I would need my head for other matters.

Another visit to my accountant, this time to discuss how to do a GST return, helped me see the road more clearly. He gave me two pieces of advice: first, if I was going to plant forestry trees I should do so as soon as possible; it would be a long term investment and the sooner I got on with planting, the quicker I'd get the return. Secondly, I should put money into renovating the farmhouse; until I was able to stay there comfortably I couldn't realise much of the house's potential. This latter point made good sense but I hadn't thought of it that way and I was pleased to have this opinion. It gave me permission to make the house liveable without feeling I was being intemperate with my limited funds.

With this guidance, I now had a much better idea of what to do. Again, I had that sense of the way ahead clearing. If I'd been religious I might have called it a revelation but to me it was the Universe offering me an opportunity I was prepared to take.

In this gradual way the farm began to change its position and purpose in my mind, becoming an economic venture and not just a fantasy I was playing out. Whilst the bulk of land would be left to regenerate into native bush, the paddocks where this would be slowest could be planted with timber trees to yield a return in the future. Generating some income from the farm made sense, if only to finance the main purpose of bush regeneration.

But there was another thing: I'd long had a vague desire to stop working and live life for its own sake rather than for the demands of my employers or the challenges of my research programmes. Now I realised that if I could make some money on the farm it might help in the distant and unformed notion of giving up work, and I wondered if this had been somewhere in the back of my mind when I'd decided to buy it.

Changing my approach to the farm meant I had to get serious about book-keeping and money matters, setting up a monthly accounting system for GST returns, recording every expenditure and filing every receipt. But although this sounds boring I didn't find it a chore — rather it was part of the adventure and I enjoyed it.

Having decided to set aside a paddock for timber trees I felt it could do no harm to have it grazed over the summer — the planting would not begin until late winter — so I called my neighbouring farmer back and said he could rent it if he still wanted to. We negotiated a price — I'd found out the going rate from the local stock agents — and my accountant was pleased to see this first trickle of income.

Now I had to decide what trees to plant. The Council had given a permit for Douglas firs but I wanted to be sure this was the most suitable species for the site and I needed a quote from a forestry company to do the planting. By chance I had a friend whose son ran just such a company on the peninsula so I arranged to meet him on the farm to get his professional advice.

He drove up in a Saab, not an ancient one like mine, but the latest model in the latest colours; clearly there was money in trees. Our having the same brand of car gave us something in common and he cheerfully chatted about trees and motors as we careered over hills and streams, inspecting my property. He soon confirmed that Douglas fir was the right choice and promised a quote in the mail for the planting.

Now I had become a farmer with serious intent and I too could worry about rainfall and rabbits and their impact on my crops. I decided to plant 5,000 trees that first winter and if I could afford it would do more the next. But for the immediate future I knew where I was going and what I was doing — some resolution had come to my life and I was happy. When the new term began I was able to throw myself into work with a renewed zest and energy. I now had a secret life which kept me going through the most boring meetings and, more importantly, I had an escape route which, although only dimly illuminated, offered a sense of hope more concrete than any fantasy in the columns of a newspaper.

It was about this time, early in the New Year, that the European visitors started arriving. First it was David, a Kiwi friend working in London, and his partner Sandi from Geneva. Both lived in exquisite, but tiny, inner-city apartments. We met at a pre-arranged spot on the road and drove together to the farm. Parking on the crest of the hill, I walked them to the highest point on the property so as to overlook the land, the bush and the views over harbour and ocean far below. The afternoon was perfect, clear of wind or cloud. We could see for miles in all directions and there wasn't a soul anywhere. Cows grazed a distant paddock, a yacht floated out at sea, we could see a couple of cottages perched on the other side of the harbour, but otherwise we were alone. For David and Sandi the contrast with their urban homes in Europe was extreme, but being adventurers and country-lovers at heart, they were readily captivated. Inevitably, when we got down to the house they were appalled by it but seemed full of confidence and enthusiasm that I would make it habitable.

A couple of weeks later another New Zealander living in London came to visit with his English wife. We picnicked outside the house looking down over the bay. Sue was pregnant with their first child and I hoped she would cope in these primitive and unsavoury conditions, but I needn't have worried; she rose to the occasion with style as we toasted both their new baby and my new farm. Dave, an electrical engineer, was fascinated by the technical problems of how to get power and water to the house, wishing he lived closer and could be involved and making me promise to keep him informed with progress reports.

These European perspectives were important boosts to my confidence. It was beginning to dawn on me that I'd taken on a fairly big task with the farm but the knowledge that others were supportive was important to keep me going. Also, I began to sense that this fantasy, to have land in the country, was a dream shared by many people and to see me realising it gave them great pleasure, particularly when their own circumstances prevented them from doing so.

One brick at a time

Picture Dee, naked from the waist up, covered in sweat and mortar and sitting astride a steep, rusty roof. We'd gone out to the farm to start taking down the chimney, something she had assured me we could do ourselves as she had lots of experience in chimney dismantling, but I didn't altogether believe her. Still, I was keen to start doing something, so on her next day off, we armed ourselves with ladder, wheelbarrow, sledge-hammer and face masks. Just getting these items down the steep hill from the car to the house was a marathon effort but it was nothing to what lay ahead.

According to Dee, there is a technique to chimney destruction which can minimise damage to bricks and to those doing the job. Basically you begin disassembling the chimney from the top and drop each brick down the inside of it. A person at the bottom removes the fallen bricks.

Dee is a lot more adventurous than I am so, inevitably, she was the one to climb onto the roof, scrabble up to the highest point and start wielding a sledge-hammer. I was the one at the bottom yelling up encouragement and standing well clear of the fireplace. I don't know how difficult she thought it would be to perch on a steeply pitched roof and swing a sledge-hammer at century-old structures but she certainly took to it with style. The mortar was so crumbly that the bricks came away as if they were held together with butter. Early on she abandoned any idea of delicately dropping each brick down the chimney. They were so easy to remove that she began tearing them off with both hands and flinging them haphazardly over the roof edge to the grass below. From there I collected them up into a tidy pile for future use.

I thought I'd opted for the safer of the two jobs, but I spent my day dodging flying bricks, bending my knees as I picked each one up, to avoid hurting my back, and shouting expletives or directions to Dee until I was hoarse with brick dust and mortar. As the sun rose and beat on the iron roof Dee got hotter and hotter. One by one she discarded her jumper and shirt, then a singlet flew off the roof and finally a bra until only the trousers remained and I still have a wonderful, if indistinct, photo of the result.

There are surprisingly many bricks in a chimney, but eventually it was down to the level of the roof and Dee made her way back to the ground, trying not to let any bare skin come in contact with the hot roof. After a quick lunch break we were into it again but this time she climbed through a trapdoor into the roof space, her small frame making the entry more easily than the builder had a few weeks earlier. The high pitch of the roof meant she could stand upright where the chimney came through the ceiling which made swinging the sledgehammer a little easier. But the air was heavy with rat remains and mortar so breathing was not pleasant.

From inside the roof Dee dropped each brick down the remaining chimney, sending out a great cloud of dust as each one landed in the fireplace. I stood in the kitchen below with the window open and waited for a gap in the flow of bricks. Then with precision timing I grabbed them from the fireplace and threw them out of the window. When enough had built up I went outside and added to my artistic stack at the side of the house.

By the end of the day the chimney was down to ceiling level and there was a substantial pile of bricks by the house. Inside, there was nothing to see of our day's hard work. But from the outside the line of the roof looked suddenly naked and misshapen. We found an old piece of corrugated iron which Dee nailed over the hole in the roof. It would keep the worst of the rain out until I got the whole roof renewed sometime in the future.

We left for home feeling filthy dirty but very satisfied. The job had proceeded without mishap — it had been easier than either of us had expected — and we'd had a good time into the bargain. This was what owning a farm was all about.

Buoyed by success and impatient to finish the job, I went back the next weekend, this time accompanied by Sue. She'd never demolished a chimney before, but being a true West Coaster, was in no doubt that she could do it. Perched on a ladder in the kitchen, she started knocking down the remaining chimney and fireplace a brick at a time while I continued removing and stacking.

The double chimney-breast housed both the large kitchen fireplace and a smaller one in the front room. Blackened and grimy from years of smoking wood, the mortar was pockmarked with cavities from which dangled pieces of straw and spiders' webs. Removing the bricks revealed a great labyrinth of nests where generations of rats had found warmth and safety.

Collections of feathers and other unimaginable ratty treasures were interspersed with desiccated skeletons still clinging onto long, rigid tails. At first we were repulsed by these remains and handled them with delicacy but by the end of the day we were pulling them out unflinchingly. It seemed these nests had been abandoned some time ago but the smell was pervasive and this, combined with the dust, made the work conditions disgusting.

But our reward was near. As the fireplaces came down, the hole between the two rooms gradually widened. Light was flooding from one room to the other. Suddenly from the kitchen we could see the ocean and realised what a beautiful space we were creating. The dark, dirty, unloved and abandoned house was coming into its own. Now it seemed full of promise; it could be a home again — warm, light and cared-for.

There was a useful lesson in all this for me. I am not good at throwing things away or disposing of unwanted possessions. I cling on as if they were part of me. To destroy any bit of an old house is not in my nature. But again the farm seemed to be on my side and was rewarding me for being brave. Pulling down the chimney, it seemed, had not damaged the essential spirit of the house, rather had revealed its exciting potential. The simple act of chimney amputation had transformed my attitude to the house. Perhaps a few other such cuts would be necessary if my life was to be similarly transformed.

None of this was in my conscious mind that night as I lay in the bath at home soaking some newly-appeared muscles. To be back in my clean and ordered house was reward in itself, as if the dirt and chaos at the farm were reminding me anew of the delights of my comfortable suburban home. I felt elated by the day's achievements and much more confident about visualising the architect's plans which he had sent through to me before going off for his summer holiday. I had asked him to try and retain the integrity of the house and its period while keeping down the building costs. He had given me a couple of options for the layout of the kitchen, living area and bathroom and had suggested a deck on the sunny side of the house, and a little portico over the front door for shelter. I can't draw even the simplest object and have no skill at converting sketches into reality, but his plans made the house look very picturesque and I tried hard to imagine which option I would like the best.

Meanwhile, at the medical school, work was winding up again after the summer break. A few people were still on leave and the students had yet to return, but there was that familiar feeling at the start of the new academic year with pressure to organise and prepare for the impending workload. There was little time or space in my head for farm matters, but I had to decide on the architect's plans so as soon as a weekend came I was off, armed with his two choices to consider on site. I persuaded Dee to come with me. She was keen to replace the broken pane in the front window which was covered with a piece of cardboard so we took putty and chisel and a sheet of glass which she'd had cut to size. The wind was blowing in strong gusts from the south but at least it wasn't raining. Still, our hands grew numb as we delicately chipped at the old putty, or rather Dee did the chipping while I played apprentice, handing her tools and keeping the putty malleable. It was the top pane and the old stool she stood on wasn't quite tall enough, so every time she stretched up a section of midriff was bared to the elements. But finally we had the glass in and just hoped the wind wouldn't pop it out before the putty set.

Inside I boiled the kettle on a camping stove and over a hot drink we contemplated the new interior. After the chimney demolition the house was looking more derelict than ever with the brick dust adding another layer of colour to the medley of dirt and insect bodies. But Dee was impressed by the light, space and views now revealed and together we considered the architect's suggestions.

The house was square; the passageway running between front and back doors had two rooms opening off each side. Each room had only one window: very sensible for heat preservation but very annoying when you longed for sunlight and views. There was no bathroom and the kitchen had a sink but no running water. I wanted to make the living room and kitchen into one, retaining two bedrooms, and I wanted a bathroom. Even more, I wanted light and plenty of access to the outside. We looked at the architect's plans. He had drawn a cutesy replica of a colonial cottage — probably very fashionable, but not in keeping with this house. Life here had been hard, cold and basic. It wasn't a place for artistic pretensions. I wanted to retain the house's functional simplicity. Any changes had to be solid and bold to match the landscape.

Dee was not impressed with the plans. She has done a bit of house designing in her time and had scorned my seeking professional advice, being sure that we could do it ourselves. So her lack of enthusiasm came as no surprise. Still, I too was uneasy with them and neither choice felt quite right. As we stood looking at the space Dee suddenly suggested moving the bedroom door here, putting the bathroom there, the sink and kitchen work space here, etc, etc. Hers was a much more sensible and creative scheme than either of the architect's and it would work. It would give me a good-sized kitchen without reducing the living space. The sink would have light and views but it wouldn't be visible from the sitting area. (I hate to be reminded of the washing-up when I'm reading). It gave a small but practicable bathroom and back bedroom. She wanted the verandah to run around three sides of the house, not be a little here and a little there as the architect suggested. But I could worry about the outside later. For now I felt pleased to have a clear solution that felt right. I was very grateful and Dee was suitably smug.

When the architect returned from holiday, I paid his bill, thanked him for his suggestions and told him he'd been helpful, which he had, in sorting out the way ahead. I didn't tell him I wouldn't be following his suggestions, but I think he suspected as much.

By now my work was building up to a frenzy again. In many ways February is the worst month in the academic's year. Each committee that has forgone a January meeting now has a doubly difficult catch-up one with a packed agenda. Students who have left enrolment until the last minute have to be interviewed and processed. I also had lectures to write, seminars to plan and research deadlines to meet. So my days at the farm were a delight by contrast. Unfortunately I was able to get away less and less but I made up for it in the evenings. Deep in thought, organising and planning the renovation of my house, I went to fewer films and concerts, rarely drank with friends and almost abandoned the dinner party circuit altogether.

But before I could begin any real building work at the farm there was one stumbling block to overcome. From the nearest parking spot to the house was a drop of about 100 metres down a steep, rough hillside. Only a rudimentary path, which had been dug up by the cattle, offered any help with the treacherous descent. I was particularly disadvantaged by this difficult access. My childhood polio, while not nearly as bad as some people's, had been serious enough to paralyse me for a year and leave me with a shortened Achilles tendon and wasted muscles in one leg. My shoes had to be built up to counteract the effect and this made going down hills quite awkward — a bit like walking around Wellington in high heels if you've ever tried that! But my discomfort wasn't the only issue with the access. Practical friends pointed out that carrying supplies and tools from trucks to house would add to the expense of building and that I might even have trouble finding a builder prepared to take it on. Before I could begin work on the house I had to put in a road.

My farming friend from the nearby bay had earlier volunteered to come and clear a track for me so now I asked for his help. He said that, by chance, the local bulldozer contractor, DC, was in the valley with his big machines and I should try and catch him as he was passing my gate. He said DC would do a much better job as he was a very skilled operator and had the proper machines. I didn't realise at the time how fortuitous this was. You could wait a couple of years for DC to be in your area. But in blissful ignorance of my luck, I called him and arranged a meeting at the farm the following weekend.

A friend, Jenny, was visiting from Auckland so she came over with me. She was clad in new white jeans, Reeboks and other 'country style' garments as designed by the fashion gurus of the city. She certainly didn't look like someone who lived in the country and I probably didn't either. We got there just before the appointed time and very soon DC turned in at the gate and sped along the track in a battered old ute, driving as if he was on a speedway. This man knew how to handle machines.

He emerged from the ute, tall and thin and taciturn with a roll-your-own hanging out the side of his mouth. I don't usually go for the macho sort but it was hard not to be impressed. DC spent half an hour deliberating, at times crashing through the undergrowth, at others contemplating the lie of the land from various perspectives. Jenny and I stood gawking like transfixed teenagers watching our pop idol. His face was battered from years of hard work, hard smoking and, I suspected, hard drinking. Yet his unhurried, silent manner had a gentleness and peacefulness that belied the elements of macho style. Then as suddenly as it had begun it was all over. Yes, it would be fine to go down through the trees. Yes, he thought there had once been a track there and it would be no problem. A boyish smile transformed his face as he jumped into the ute and waved goodbye, promising to begin the job the next Thursday.

Friends in town were following my progress with the farm and our social times were often dominated now by accounts of my successes, such as the chimney demolition, or of my headaches — like how to improve access to the house. Johnny Johnson, a retired roading engineer, had recently visited the farm and walked all its tracks with me. He had initially suggested the route that DC had agreed to make, linking the farm track and the house through the trees.

On the day DC was to start the track Johnny came out to the farm too, as interested as I was to see how the work would proceed. We'd only just arrived and opened the thermos of tea when we heard the low throb of an engine somewhere in the distance. For a long time nothing was visible until, creeping steadily up the road, came a huge digger outlined against the bush. Finally it reached my gate and turned along the track towards us. The size and power of the machine was overwhelming. I was impressed and scared at the same time.

DC jumped down from the cab to exchange a few words, but he was soon back in his seat and beginning the job. I took up a position high above the work area with a good view of proceedings but well out of the way. Where the track was to branch down to the house it needed to be widened. So DC began eating away at the hillside above the track, dropping earth where the road was to go down. Very soon he had enough of a base to take the machine over the edge. Looking as though it was being driven over a precipice, the digger just lurched over a little then began laboriously taking earth from the side of the hill and building up the road in front, gradually edging itself down and evening up as it went. In just a couple of hours DC had the digger almost to the back door. Where there had been only a tangle of trunks, branches and creepers down a steep gully there was now a clear track. Its line curved naturally along the hillside then swept down to the house through an avenue of macrocarpa pines. Now it was obvious that there'd been a road here before — it fitted so snugly the lie of the land, and the archway of trees, although battered and broken from years of wild weather, stood sentry-like, announcing the entrance to a secret world.

I recalled my Northumberland childhood in the rectory at the end of a long drive of centuries-old elm trees known locally as the twelve apostles. In spring their feet were covered in purple and gold crocuses while in autumn their leaves formed huge drifts across the drive. This track had nothing like the softness and civilized air of that entranceway, but it gave me a sense of familiarity and comfort along with joy at the ease of access it would give me. I couldn't yet bring my car down, but the form was there and I could clearly see how it would develop.

Over lunch that day DC and Johnny chatted easily in the monosyllabic and verbless way that men do who are used to working alone and outside. I was jangling and gauche, ill-fitted to this company and overexcited by the progress of the morning. I offered them too many cups of tea and fussed over the sugar bowl whose contents had become solid through lack of use. These men were used to diggers and what could be achieved by them. They were blasé about their power to change the shape of the land with the whim of their lever-driving fingers. I was both impressed and saddened. Nothing seemed to be sacred; they could move even mountains.

Of course I said nothing of this but was hearty and jolly and impressed by what had been achieved so far, however DC cautioned me that this had been the easy bit and that the tidying up and surfacing of the road would be a much slower process. Still, when I returned to the farm a few days later I watched him put the finishing touches to the track and then tidy up the turning area which he encircled with huge boulders unearthed during the course of the job. He still had some loads of gravel to lay but the road itself was complete. On my next visit I could, for the first time, drive to within metres of my back door.

The dreaded weed

Do I believe in angels? I'm not sure, but when David Webster came into my life I was desperately in need of one, and though he arrived in a green Volkswagon rather than a heavenly chariot, it seemed as though something, or someone, ethereal must be looking after me. It was April and I'd struck my first major crisis with the farm and was feeling powerless, alone and vulnerable. My ignorance in farming matters was beginning to hit home and none of my city friends could help. The problem wasn't catastrophic like a land slip or a volcanic eruption, it was something that had crept up on me stealthily and silently. The problem was gorse. You may think I'm being a bit emotional to label a mere plant a crisis, but by the time I met David that was how large the problem had become.

Since my first day of owning the farm I'd known I had to do something about gorse, but I'd managed to keep the worry at bay, finding it more exciting to focus on the house renovation or the tree planting. But now the problem could no longer be ignored as the gorse on the hillsides, unnoticed by me for months, began its autumn flowering and turned the land bright yellow. With this came another call from the Regional Council's noxious weeds officer to ask when I was going to remove it. I couldn't put the problem aside any longer.

A few months earlier I'd known nothing about gorse but by now I'd learnt it was a major headache to many of the farmers on the peninsula. Brought in from Scotland last century, it's a very invasive shrub in this climate, taking hold wherever it can find a break in the pasture and expanding to cover the land, making it impenetrable and useless for grazing. Although it flowers only once a year in its native country, here in New Zealand gorse has two seasons, giving us twice as many seeds to contend with and they can lie dormant in the soil for years before sprouting up as soon as conditions allow.

The Regional Council has legally designated it a 'noxious weed' on Banks Peninsula and makes us clear all the gorse within ten metres of our boundaries and any scattered patches in paddocks. The job of the noxious weeds officer is to see that the rules are upheld and, if not, you can be taken to court and given a hefty fine — something that happened to previous owners of my farm. So the consequences of my inaction could be serious.

But the story is more complicated than this. If gorse is enemy number one to the Council, it is not so to Hugh on the nearby reserve — he loves it! For him it is the most versatile and beneficial of plants, acting as a nursery crop for the regeneration of native vegetation. Natives find it hard to re-establish in pasture-covered land but when gorse takes over and has grown tall enough, it opens up and lets in the light, allowing any native seeds present to germinate and grow in the nitrogen-enriched soil. While its painful thorns keep away browsing animals, the gorse gives shelter to the young plants which, in time, when they grow big enough to form a thick canopy, smother the gorse, preventing its seedlings from establishing and allowing the native vegetation to dominate.

On my farm I wanted the gorse for regeneration purposes but I was legally obliged to keep the boundaries and open spaces clear of it — several hectares of pasture and miles of fence-lines. Thousands of plants had to be destroyed. For someone whose previous experience of weed control amounted to dealing with rogue convolvulus amongst the roses, this was a big ask! How to deal with gorse became a pre-occupation that grew triffid-like in my mind just as the gorse did on my pastures. If I'd been grazing the land perhaps I could have resorted to spraying it, but I was caught in a dilemma; the same sprays that killed the gorse would kill the natives I was trying to regenerate.

Swearing never to use sprays, Hugh had developed various other methods of killing gorse which he offered to teach me. Very small plants can be pulled out by their roots, if you wear leather gloves to avoid the prickles, but larger ones must be dug out carefully to minimise disruption to the soil and so prevent germination of more seeds. When the plants are too big for this you can cut through the stem and immediately paint the cut with chemicals which are absorbed into the plant and kill it. These methods may all sound easy but I found them laborious, painful and time-consuming.

Hugh's lessons were helpful but they served to emphasise the problems I faced and made me even more depressed. Living on his reserve full-time, maybe Hugh could conquer his unwanted gorse in this way but it wouldn't work for me with only Saturday visits. Much as I wanted to follow his example, I decided that pragmatism rather than conservation had to define my course of action and I would have to get the gorse sprayed. Perhaps in following years I would have a better strategy organised.

I arranged to meet a local weed contractor on the farm to get a quote and agree on the areas to be sprayed. As I drove over from Christchurch that day my mood had none of the joy and sense of escapade which usually characterised visits to the farm and it didn't improve when the weed man arrived. He drove up in a dilapidated old farm truck which looked as though it had done one too many years of hard service, as did the dog who jumped down from the back. We exchanged the normal opening pleasantries but from there on our conversation went downhill.

Depressing and negative, the man made me feel I had the worst gorse on the peninsula. As we walked together over the land, he pointed out the numerous little shoots sprouting up undetected by my ignorant eye, and he impressed on me the enormity of the problem I faced. Completely dismissive of my plans to regenerate native bush, he told me how previous owners had done so well, through hard work and good management, at keeping out the gorse — implying that I, an outsider and non-farmer, was unlikely to come up to this standard. He quoted $2,000 to spray the main paddock but warned this would have little effect because of all the young gorse coming through. Only by heavy grazing of the land would I get rid of the small shoots hidden in the grass and without this it would cost more and more each year to control the gorse.

I left him and my yellow hillsides as soon as I could and escaped back to the comfort and solidity of a city house where plants knew their place and nature didn't rule. With several glasses of wine I tried, unsuccessfully, to drown out the unpalatable diagnosis and the unpleasant prospect of trying to find thousands of dollars each year just to kill plants. But there was no escape. I hadn't liked the man and I hadn't liked his news but, reluctantly, I saw the logic of his advice and the impossibility of the situation I was in.

The paddock of concern had once been covered with gorse so the earth was filled with its seeds. Previous owners had cleared it gradually and kept it heavily stocked with sheep so that they ate any young shoots as they appeared. Now that I'd had nothing grazing there for four months the gorse was coming up everywhere, so extensively that it would be impossible to keep down with spraying alone — even if I could afford it. Only with the help of browsing stock could I hope to control it.

But I didn't want this — how could the natives regenerate if they were being eaten back all the time? The problem seemed insurmountable — I didn't want any stock and I couldn't sustain $2,000 a year for spraying, but if I didn't control the gorse I could be taken to court and the resulting fine could be much larger.

While I was beginning to despair, I was also getting frustrated by the Council's ruling. I was prepared to keep my boundaries free of gorse to protect my neighbours from its spread, but I couldn't see the justice in them controlling what I grew elsewhere — what I chose to do in the privacy of my own paddocks! I wanted this land, not for pasture, but to have it return to native bush and the best way for this to happen was to let the gorse invade it completely so that the natives would come through. Perhaps with time I could sort it out but, right now, the noxious weeds officer and the gorse were equally relentless in their pursuit and time was running out.

It was at this point of desperation that the angel turned up. David Webster was the local field officer for the QEII Trust for Conservation, a body I hadn't heard of before, but the 50 acres of native bush on my land was covenanted to the Trust which meant, according to my lawyer, that it was legally set aside for conservation and must be kept fenced from stock. When I got the call from their field officer to say he would like to meet me and inspect the covenanted land I was a bit nervous, as if the auditor or the school inspector was coming for his annual visit.

At exactly the appointed time a dark green VW Beetle parked at the farm gate and a man started down the track to the house. As I went up to meet him I saw a tall lean figure in his fifties in well-cut jeans and a fashionable navy Aran jumper. I don't know what I'd been expecting but it wasn't this. In my ratty house he seemed a bit too clean to sit at the improvised table and stools, but I needn't have worried. Quickly producing sandwiches and a thermos of coffee, he set about lunch with gusto while telling me all about the QEII Trust and our mutual responsibilities.

I liked David immediately. He was interested in my plans, encouraging and enthusiastic, but more than anything else, he was helpful. Suddenly I was no longer alone with my gorse problem and I began to see the implications of having a QEII covenant — I had a partner in the conservation work which was a major government-funded body with staff and resources. I couldn't expect big grants from them, but they would offer support and expertise. Over the years I was to become more and more grateful for David's efficient, quiet and determined help. He would write letters, call people and talk to contacts. Without ruffling feathers or causing upsets he would get things done. But that day it was a huge relief to talk over the gorse problem with someone who not only sympathised but took it on board as a shared concern.

Striding over the paddock with him, I explained the problem, which he understood at once — he'd been a farmer and knew the value of sheep in keeping down young gorse, as well as the costs and 'collateral damage' of sprays. He agreed that it was counter-productive to keep this paddock free of gorse when I wanted it to regenerate, and said he would talk to the Council and try to get their permission to let it revert. In the meantime, he suggested I graze it for a month or so to get over the immediate problem.

Feeling a great weight lift off my shoulders, I now knew what to do. Calling my farmer neighbour, I asked if he would put his sheep in the paddock for a time at no charge and he was only too happy to oblige. Then I wrote to the Council asking permission to let the paddock go back to gorse for bush regeneration, quoting the scientific evidence of Hugh's work next door to prove the value of this. It was some months before I received their letter of approval and stopped dreading the call from the noxious weeds officer and began to enjoy my visits to the farm again.

Now, as I write this chapter, I wonder if I've been able to fully convey the despair and anxiety that this episode caused me. Even today, gorse can still give me sleepless nights, but I have it more in perspective and understand why it caused me so much grief in that first year. My real problem with gorse was not with the Council, its noxious weeds officer or even with the dreary weed sprayer. The problem of gorse was one of control. I was quite powerless in the face of its relentless growth. No matter how much spray I might throw at it or how many hours I might spend on my knees pulling it out, I couldn't prevent it coming up. I could slow down its expansion, but I couldn't stop it. It was in control of me, not the other way round.

I wouldn't have described myself as a control freak but nevertheless this degree of powerlessness was difficult to accept. At that time in my life the basics such as heat, light and sound were available on demand. Technology and transport were reliable, any failures were quickly fixed, and when I had problems with staff or students at work they were solved. I wasn't used to being beaten by things or people, let alone by plants.

Looking back I can see that all this worry with the gorse was yet another step on the road to escape from city life. It was a test of my suitability for life in the country and it was one I might easily have failed if it hadn't been for the divine intervention of David and the QEII Trust. But now, several years on, I acknowledge the power of nature over people. Now I live in a place where people are small fry, where the market economy and its obsession with choice is irrelevant to the forces of wind and weather, and where those who are genuinely happy have learnt to live with the elements of nature, not just to exercise dominance over them.

Ironically, I now see gorse as an asset to the farm, not only for helping the bush to regenerate, but in lots of other ways. The perfume is superb, like coconut and frangipani combined, so a walk through the paddocks in bloom-time can be like a visit to a tropical paradise. When no others are around, I use the flowers to decorate tables. Their yellow vibrancy promises summer or snow, depending on your mood. And they cheer up my cooking — gorse flower scones in winter, gorse and grapefruit marmalade to wake up the overnight guests and gorse liqueur to send them to sleep again! Pressed gorse flowers embellish the walking sticks and dead gorse trunks burn in the fire. And then there are its healing powers. According to Bach's *Flower Remedies*, gorse is a great antidote for depression, but as such I haven't needed to try it yet!

Finding Andy

'*Re-piling*' isn't a very appealing word nor is it an interesting aspect of house renovation, but that is what the architect had told me I must tackle first. Knowing nothing about piles I had to ask Dee for an explanation. Apparently piles are the chunks of wood or concrete which buildings sit on to take them off the ground and keep them level. With time some of the piles can sink and need replacing to get the building back to plumb.

The farmhouse piles were made from totara, a local hardwood, and they'd been in the ground for 100 years. Replacing them wasn't something I could contemplate doing myself and it was even beyond the skills of Dee, so I would have to get it done by a professional builder. I'd noticed that when you mentioned the need for 're-piling', people sympathised and spoke in hushed, almost funereal tones, as if it was the worst thing a home-owner could face, so I was prepared for a fairly big bill, probably in the thousands rather than the hundreds. Getting a couple of quotes from local builders would soon tell me how many months' salary I'd be up for.

The first man to come was pleasant, efficient and expensive — so expensive that I wouldn't be able to do anything more to the house for a year! The next was unpleasant, inefficient — he turned up on the wrong day — but at least he was cheaper.

Neither of them seemed right. I didn't want to use a costly firm for the sake of a name nor have a bad job for the sake of a few dollars. So I kept looking and asking around for suggestions.

A friend in Christchurch mentioned a couple who'd recently moved to the peninsula to renovate a house and said maybe their builder would be good. It was worth a try so one Saturday I set off to find them down a long road in a nearby bay. Luckily they were home and showed me round their house, but as they'd done all the work on it themselves, not using a builder, they couldn't offer any advice. Then they remembered a neighbour in the bay who was a builder — they didn't know whether he was any good but he was a nice bloke and they suggested I try him for a quote. It was in this serendipitous and unceremonious way that my association with Andy began — one that was to run through several years and many thousands of dollars, and leave me forever admiring his skills.

Andy turned out to be a chef cum builder cum furniture maker — a quintessential New Zealander who could do anything and solve any problem with a combination of lateral thinking, confidence and a good dose of optimism. When I phoned he willingly agreed to meet me at the farm and give me a quote for the re-piling.

He arrived in an old white Transit van which he manoeuvred expertly down the drive before opening the doors to let out two small boys and one large Labrador. I was to learn that Andy was one of those rare men who could do more than one thing at once, so a visit to my farm to quote on a job was also an opportunity to exercise the dog, entertain the children and pick up the supplies from Akaroa on the way home.

I liked him at once. He was a small, compact man with an enviably olive complexion, sparkling eyes and a rosy smile. Assuring me that re-piling would be no problem, he said it was just like changing a tyre on your car: you jacked up one side of the house, removed the old piles, put in new ones and let the house down again. Repeat this on all sides and the job was done. There was no attempt to mystify me or impress me with tales of what a difficult task it would be and consequently how expensive. On the contrary, he made it sound so easy that it wouldn't take long at all and his quote reflected that confidence.

I seemed to have found the builder I could work with and drove back to the city in a glow of optimism. The way was now clear to begin the first stage of renovation and, although I didn't realise it at the time, the farmhouse had met up with its saviour.

A couple of weeks later Andy did the re-piling, helped by his friend Chris, the wood-turner. When he rang me to report on progress, he seemed excited by their achievements and keen to show off the result, sounding almost like a child who's built his first model plane. I couldn't imagine what would be exciting about re-piling but I was anxious to see what they'd done so I met him at the farm on the first chance I had.

It was a bright, clear autumn day as I drove in the gate and down to the house. Andy had warned me that it had needed quite a bit of levelling but I was unprepared for the change. Previously the house had settled into the earth, snuggling into the bank behind and looking as if it was slowly returning to the bush from which it had come. Now it sat proudly and squarely facing out to sea, no longer slumped into the hill, but alive to the challenges ahead.

I had no idea how out-of-line the house had become or what a difference the re-piling would make to the feel of the place. In one corner it was about a foot higher and instead of a sloping passageway from the back to the front door there was now a level and secure route. Lifted slightly off the ground, the house had a light and airy look as if it had just landed from outer space to rest on its little round piles. Inside it was still draughty and dirty, but somehow it looked as though it was on the road to recovery. It was like straightening the tie of a drunken businessman; although he still can't walk properly, at least he looks as though he knows what direction he's going in!

So the first steps in the renovation had been taken and I was filled with enthusiasm and energy to get on with the next. I asked Andy if he'd do more; I'd compiled a long list of building and plumbing jobs which seemed daunting, perhaps not to him, but certainly to me, the keeper of the cheque book. But Andy was cheerful and optimistic, suggesting we do things a stage at a time. If I ran out of money we would just stop the work and wait till I'd earned a bit more.

I'd had the farm about six months by now and it may seem that, apart from chimney demolition, my contribution had been limited to making phone calls and paying the occasional bill but, on the contrary, I'd been very busy. Having decided on how to redesign the house, I'd had to find all the building requirements such as doors and windows. Fortunately, Christchurch is a heaven of demolition yards and for months I'd spent my lunch hours haunting these places. While the others at work rushed to the gym for their daily exercise, I jumped in my car and sped to the seedier parts of town to pick over old house bits.

I enjoy demolition yards and revel in the hopes and dreams that their wares conjure up. You can be looking for a square window with six panes but fall in love with a totally impractical bay window that is twice the size you need. Whole houses have been redesigned or rebuilt to accommodate little love affairs of this sort. I had quite a precise list of requirements but still I lingered in the yards, flirting with completely unsuitable items and my hour-long lunches could easily become stretched to two or more without my having eaten a thing.

If I'd had a meeting in the morning or given a lecture, I'd be dressed appropriately, probably in something that tried to marry femininity with serious intent, but these weren't the best clothes for touring demolition yards. I'd curse the padded shoulders, so fashionable at the time, as I tried to squeeze through gaps between collections of old doors and windows and my dry-cleaning bill began to reflect my nefarious lunchtimes. I don't know what the men in these yards thought when this figure of what tried to be understated elegance picked through their piles of junk, but they were always helpful and cheery. Perhaps to demolition men, saving building materials is akin to saving souls and produces that same radiance and joy that you see on nuns' faces.

The most important item on my list was a pair of French doors for the main entrance to the house from the drive. I wanted them to let in the light and views but not to spoil the basic simplicity of the façade. So I looked for doors which were of the right era, about 100 years old, but not too elegant or large. Early on I struck gold with a pair of fully restored kauri doors in a frame for $450. Quite narrow, they wouldn't overwhelm the room and were simple in design, made up of three panels with the top two glassed and the bottom one wooden. They were exactly what I wanted but I put them on hold and asked Dee to go and inspect them, not entirely trusting my visualising abilities. 'Perfect and very tinny!' she said, 'You could have searched for years and had to pay three times the price!' The doors stayed in the yard until I was ready to collect them some months later, and by then the man said he could have sold them a hundred times over.

For the bathroom I found a long, thin window, just the size to let me look out at the bush as I lay in the perfect bath. That was deep and narrow and would provide me with long hot soaks without using the entire tank of hot water. A tiny corner handbasin, just big enough to clean your teeth over without taking up precious space, and a small square shower tray completed what I needed for that room. Then I found exactly the right window to replace the back door; it was large and four-paned, identical to the existing windows so that when it was installed it looked as though it had been part of the original house. Finally, I got another pair of French doors, small and sturdy, to open out onto the sunny side of the house.

Searching for the ideal log-burning stove involved visiting all the heating shops in Christchurch which, as winter approached, became a more and more appealing task. As well as heating the house and water, the stove had to have a cooking top and must fit in aesthetically, although I kept telling myself this shouldn't be a priority. Just as you're not supposed to buy a car for its colour I felt I shouldn't buy a stove because of its look. But in the end I was lucky here too. The one stove I loved the look of, the appropriately named 'Lady Kitchener', was also the one that best fitted my requirements and that the salesmen strongly recommended.

It came in a range of colours: sky blue, bottle green or deep maroon — all great — but I was leaning towards the green, probably in an attempt to blend it with the trees and grass outside the house. I asked my artist friend Sue what she thought but she said no, she'd go for the blue. You wanted the inside of the house to feel warm and cosy, not a part of the bush, particularly not when it was freezing outside. So I got the blue, a colour I'd never much liked before since I'm neither blonde nor into denim, but it was the beginning of an ongoing affair. I still don't buy clothes in blue, but living with it around me has become addictive. Mirroring the sky, it gives warmth or coolness depending on the requirements and it gives a glow to bare wooden boards as no other colour can.

While I'd been having such success in my search for these building things, back at the farm Mother Nature was about to tip the balance the other way. Before Andy could begin the inside work we had to weatherproof the house which meant putting on a new roof and some guttering. I'd got a few quotes in and agreed to that of a specialist company in Christchurch who gave us a date for the job and Andy scheduled the building work to start after that. On the appointed day, sometime in June, the weather was not kind and the roofers bailed out. I felt sympathetic; putting up a roof in high winds is not safe, but their schedule was so tight that the next available date was about six weeks away. This was a blow to our plans. We couldn't put the log-burner in before the roof was on and Andy was reluctant to do too much of the inside work before the house was leak-proof. But he was philosophical, he'd had plenty of experience of delays caused by weather, and we just waited for the rescheduled date.

It got to be mid-July when the weather was at its coldest and ever less appealing to the roofing company, so the job was further delayed. Then Andy came up with a solution: he and Chris would do the roofing for the same price as the quote and we would buy all the materials from the company as agreed. Everyone was happy — I suspect the company's contractors were relieved not to have to tackle the job — and Andy could now get on with it.

I went to the roofing suppliers and paid for the materials and later that day Andy came to Christchurch, stacked his big white van with metres of corrugated iron and guttering and headed back to the peninsula. Now all we wanted was clear weather for a day or two; working on a steep roof in rain or snow would be lethal and sheets of iron in high winds can whip around and cut you with the speed of a guillotine.

The forecast looked good for later in the week so we scheduled in the job. It was mid-term break at medical school so I could get away from work for the day and at least offer moral support to Andy, if not anything practical. As I drove over in the morning, the weather was fine so things looked promising. I'd set off fairly early and decided to stop in Akaroa for a coffee to wake up and warm up before heading to the farm. Pulling up outside a café I saw Andy and his wife Sarah sitting having breakfast. They waved warmly but something was odd — I'd expected Andy to be on the roof by now. Joining them, I was greeted with the news that the timing might be right for the roofing but it was also right for the baby they were expecting. Sarah had gone into labour that night and they'd come over to the hospital in the early hours. Now things had slowed down and the midwife had let them go down to the village for breakfast. So we sat together over coffee as Sarah coped with the first stages of labour. All thoughts of roofing were abandoned as I joined in the spirit of helping their baby into the world.

As it turned out, things didn't go well in the birthing department. The weather deteriorated, the labour got complicated and Sarah had to endure a stormy helicopter transfer to the base hospital in Christchurch while Andy sped along in his car trying to match its pace. A most beautiful baby eventuated but not without considerable stress to both parents.

Once things had settled down with the new baby Andy was keen to get back to work but now winter had set in properly and he worried that his van, laden with roofing iron, might not make it along the farm track. I arranged for a local farmer to come up with a tractor and transport things from the gate but on the day I had to sit through a stodgy meeting at work while several people battled the elements to get my roofing iron, building materials, log-burner and bath to the house. Dee went over with a friend, Sally, and together with Andy and the farmer they pushed and pulled through sleet and mud till everything was safely there. Even the tractor had difficulty at one stage and poor Sally, who'd been told she was going out for a nice day in the country, was ill-prepared for the task, but even if she was exhausted and freezing her dog had a great time.

Hardly stopping to draw breath, Andy and Chris began roofing the next day and by the weekend they had it complete.

I went over to see it and again met an excited Andy anxious to show me the changes. As soon as I caught sight of the house the difference was clear. Instead of the rusty old tin-shed effect, we now had a shiny solid roof with guttering and downpipes and the house looked as if it could almost be inhabited by humans rather than cows! We discussed the next jobs; now it all seemed to be happening and I was keen to be involved in as much as I could.

At work my colleagues spent their weekends on the local ski fields or took a week's break from the winter in Fiji, while I travelled relentlessly back and forth to Akaroa to watch my farm slowly materialize. I didn't attempt to stay the night again after that first freezing and frightening one, but always drove there and back in a day or bedded down at my friends' house in the valley.

Once Andy got going he moved fast. First he put in the French doors which gave light and access to the main room and a wonderful vista up the drive. Next it was the log-burner and hot water cylinder. He made a beautiful cupboard to house the cylinder by reusing the old totara weatherboards that had been cut out to make way for the new doors. These were planed and finished until they shone with the glow of old wood and the cupboard was put at an angle to the room by recessing it into the corner. Next Andy tackled the bathroom, where everything fitted exactly as hoped, then he replaced the back door with the window, and re-hung the old door in place of one missing from the bedroom.

Real progress was being made and as winter drew to a close I felt there was a definite possibility the farm would be habitable by summer.

Only an idiot

After I'd lived several years on the farm, when the house was open to the public for a garden tour, a woman arrived who'd looked at the property when it was for sale. 'I told the agent only an idiot would buy this!' she said as she was introduced to me. Another visitor, an ex-neighbour of the farm, said he'd thought I was some sort of New Age nutter when I took it on, and I'm sure these two weren't the only ones speculating about my sanity.

As the outward appearance of the farm began to change, I expect the size and variety of the tales about its new owner grew too. It must have seemed a bit strange to the locals that the old farmhouse, derelict for 60 years, was now having money lavished upon it, while the fertile land, grazed intensively for 100 years, was being left to revert to bush and the dreaded gorse. There was plenty for people to talk about. Who knows what stories went round, but the word 'crazy' probably featured in many of them and a bit of poetic licence will have crept in too. But one day, towards the end of winter, I gave the locals a genuine reason for a laugh or two.

Andy was ready to begin the plumbing and I'd offered to get the required bits and pieces in the city; Dee had a contact in the plumbing industry so I'd get a good price. We arrived at the plumber's yard one Saturday and were soon surrounded by a vast conglomeration of pipes, connectors, lagging, adhesives and tapes. How to get them to the farm was beyond me — they were far too long to fit in my car — but Dee was as resourceful as ever. She strapped the lengths of pipe onto the roof and put all the other bits and pieces in the back with the three dogs. I drove off cautiously, peering out through the small gap between the bonnet and the collection of pipe ends secured to the front bumper.

In Christchurch it was cold and clear with bright sunshine but approaching the farm we found a thick layer of fresh snow; winter had not yet left the upper reaches of the peninsula. The main road had been cleared but the smaller one leading to the farm gate defeated me. I couldn't get enough traction to get up the last steep incline and I had no snow chains. Being only half a mile from our destination, we couldn't bear to go all the way back to the city without delivering the cargo. Dee is not one to be beaten by a bit of snow and she soon had a scheme worked out. If it hadn't been so cold I might have been more sceptical, as I usually am of her 'brilliant suggestions', but that day I just went along with her.

The dogs were released from the car and rushed about yelping with glee, rolling and falling in the white powder. Taking all the pipes off the roof, we tied them into long bundles attached to our waists and began trudging through the snow, pulling them behind us, our arms laden with the associated bits and pieces. The snow was deep and it was hard work — my legs don't have much strength for that sort of thing and I was falling behind. After a time Dee suggested we use some of the dog power available, so we put them on leads, tied lengths of pipe and bags of bits behind them, and tried to get them to pull their share. My Vita was quite good at the job; as a Tibetan terrier she'd been bred for conditions like this, and Dee's border collie Jessie was passively obliging, but her Great Dane Bess was not at all cooperative. Breaking free from our hold, she went charging up the road, scattering plumbing bits all over the snow, trying desperately to rid herself of the evil black pipe following behind! It was about this time that some neighbours appeared, slowly edging past us in their four-wheel drive. I didn't know them but I could tell what they were thinking from the expressions on their faces and I knew that another story of that mad woman was now going to be doing the rounds of the locals.

We managed to collect up all the precious bits and carry on, embarrassed but undeterred, though we abandoned ideas of help from the dogs. With snowdrifts well above our knees in some places, the progress was slow, but we finally made it to the house and got everything deposited safely inside. A toboggan was going to be essential transport for winters!

Seeing the farm in snow for the first time was magical; even the house was transformed into a picture book beauty. Silence hung heavily in the stillness, the birds were subdued, the light blinding and the tall trees of the bush stood up like green sentries above their broad white skirts. It was as if we'd stepped into an English Christmas card, only the scene was wilder and more dramatic. This was probably the first time I appreciated the utter contrast between one side of the peninsula and the other. Here on the eastern extremities the severity of snow and sense of isolation almost mimicked those of Mt Cook, yet down at the harbour, only ten minutes away, people were strolling around in T-shirts, or enjoying a coffee in the sun.

Captivated by the beauty and atmosphere of the farm, we were almost oblivious to the cold, but our feet and clothes were soaked from frequent falls in the snow and even a drink heated on the camp stove couldn't warm us through. Reluctantly retracing our steps — it was easier and safer to use our footprints as a pathway — we finally got back to the car and drove home with the heater on full throttle, returning to a city quite unaware of the Antarctic-like conditions just an hour's drive away.

But the mission was accomplished and with the plumbing requirements on site, all was now ready for Andy to begin connecting them up. I'd decided not to use the spring for water; it needed to be dug, cleared out and have pipes laid underground. I'd just collect rainwater from the roof and store it in a large tank. In such a high rainfall area this seemed a simpler solution and I could add in the spring at a later date if necessary.

Plumbing has always been a bit of a mystery to me but Andy reckoned it would only take us a day. I was to act as his apprentice; he needed someone to help him and I wanted to see it put together and to understand how it worked. He explained the whole system: the pipes were of varying diameters according to the pressure of the water passing through them and those for hot water were made of copper while the rest were heavy-duty plastic. The cold water had to come from the tank to feed taps in the bathroom and kitchen and supply the cylinder, the hot water came from the cylinder to its taps and then we had to take the waste water from the various outlets.

Despite Andy's explanation it seemed complicated but he was reassuring and patient, as ever.

It was a dull day but not too cold when I escaped from work to meet Andy at the farm. He'd already been on the job for an hour when I arrived and was well under way. He worked at impressive speed and we soon had pipes running all over the place. While Andy spent most of the time squeezed underneath the house on his back to join, tack and saw, I cut the pipes to length according to his instructions, handed him tools and fed long lines of piping to him. Once or twice I had to join him lying on my back amongst the dirt and accumulated debris of the last century, holding a pipe in position. The first time was the worst, as I imagined the rat dung and spiders' webs in my hair, but soon I was past caring and slid along on my back using bent legs as propellants. I could never match Andy's carefree action, but I became fairly good at the under house back crawl!

By the end of the day the work was all but complete. We still had to lag the pipes under the house and dig in the ones to go underground, but these were labouring jobs that could be done any time; the basic plumbing was finished. With a dramatic gesture, Andy turned on the tap from the outside tank and produced running water inside the house for the first time in its 100 year history. The success of the day was slightly marred by the hot water system not working — there was water in the cylinder, it just wasn't coming out of the taps — but it was too late to try and sort that one out. For now we were both content with our achievements which, to me, seemed quite considerable.

Now that I live on the farm full-time, my water supply comes

Handyman's Dream: Dee inspects the soon-to-be-demolished chimney.

Getting tools down to the house: the author at full-throttle.

Andy and Chris unload building supplies in midwinter,
helped by Simon, a neighbouring farmer.

The transplanted kitchen unit.

Andy proudly displays the tank and passive heating system of the composting toilet.

Looking down over Akaroa harbour
from the high point on Cloud Farm.

Boulders, ferns and fuchsia trunks form
a natural garden at the side of the house.

from the spring rather than the skies. I managed on rainwater for some years but one particularly dry summer gave me the incentive I needed to get the spring dug out and linked up. Now there is never a shortage of water and I even have taps all over the garden and a little waterfall by the house transforming the spring's overflow into a thing of beauty. Occasionally the pipes freeze in winter but, apart from that, I have a continuous flow of pure spring water straight from its source.

But that first year, in my naivety and ignorance, I opted for the simplicity of rainwater and this turned out to be behind the problem we'd encountered getting the hot water to run. Andy took no time to figure it out: we'd made a mistake in our calculations about the height of the rain storage tank in relation to the hot water cylinder. It wasn't high enough to fill the cylinder to the level of the outflow. This called for a fairly major solution. We couldn't change the position of the cylinder as it was fixed at a particular angle to the stove for the water to heat correctly; nor could we change the rainwater tank because putting it any higher would take it above the level of the guttering that collected the rain.

Andy's suggestion was to put in another tank a bit higher up the hill, filling it by pumping from the rainwater tank. In the longer term, I hoped to build a garage above the house, from which we could take water off the roof to fill the top tank, but in the meantime, Andy would lend me a pump and generator and once a fortnight or so I would have to transfer water from the bottom to the top tank.

Off I went to the farming supply store where I bought the largest tank they had in stock and, with the help of a couple of burly assistants, managed to wedge it inside the cage of my borrowed trailer. Setting off for the farm, I looked like a snail with a monstrous shell on my back and I hoped that the strong winds along the way would not catch and overturn the load. I picked up Dee en route and we made it to the farm without incident. Getting the tank out of the trailer was a bit difficult but we managed and somehow got it down the hill and into position. Fortunately there was a ledge in just the right place so no major earthworks were required and the tank settled in snugly, looking as if it had always been there.

Next we had to cut a hole near its bottom to fit the outlet pipe and this involved one of us getting inside the tank to screw it in. Dee gets a bit claustrophobic so I was volunteered for the job. Getting in was easy; I just dropped through the hole in the top, but once the task was complete I found I couldn't get out again, much to Dee's amusement. No matter how many times she encouraged me to jump and pull myself up by my arms, I was just not strong enough, and the more we laughed the weaker I got. Now, after several more tank installations around the property, I have learnt that you put a tank on its side to climb into it — and get out again just as easily. But my mind doesn't work that strategically so I found myself in a predicament that gave Dee a great photo and a big laugh at my expense. Fortunately we thought of a creative solution before I was sentenced to a night standing upright in a black polyethylene tank. Dee found a small stool which could be passed through the hole, provided I was bent double inside the tank. By standing on this, I managed to haul myself out, pulling the stool behind me with the piece of string she had tied to its leg. My childhood devotion to puzzle books had finally paid off!

I'll never know whether she deliberately set me up or if she, too, was inexperienced in working with water tanks!

When I next met Andy at the farm he connected the two tanks, pumped the top one full and, as he'd predicted, the problem was solved. With the cylinder full of water we could at last start up the log-burner — a momentous occasion. Packing the hot box with paper and wood, Andy ceremoniously lit it, then the two of us stood around exclaiming at the resultant warmth as if we'd discovered fire for the first time. It was probably more of a miracle for him than for me — he'd had to work there in the coldest days of winter, whereas I'd always had the option to go home when the temperature got too cold. As warmth filled the room it transformed the house into a liveable place.

Keeping the warmth in was the next job and this meant insulating the ceiling. I'd found some soft woollen batts, nicer than the usual fibreglass ones, which were delivered to my garage in Christchurch and from there I transported the huge cigar-shaped bundles to the farm one at a time whenever I visited.

Dee offered to help with laying them in the ceiling and, though I'd never done it before, I assumed it would be a relatively pleasant and easy job. Perhaps I should have been alarmed when she loaded the car with stepladder, buckets, brushes and face masks, but I was used to her overzealous planning and noticed nothing particularly unusual. We got out to the farm quite early and immediately lit the log-burner, unable to resist the novelty of fire even though the day promised to be warm.

The first challenge was getting into the roof space through a large hole in the ceiling where the chimney used to be, using Dee's rickety old stepladder. At ten feet high the ladder didn't quite match the twelve foot height of the ceiling. Dee, of course, managed the gap easily by attaching a rope to hold onto and yanking herself up. But when I tried, it was a different matter; this potentially lethal manoeuvre terrified me with my weak arms and horror of unstable footings. Encouraging me from above, Dee managed at last to get me up, though once I was there, she burst out laughing at my purple lips and trembling arms. Getting down was going to be even worse but for the moment I concentrated on the job at hand.

Before we could begin to lay the insulation we had to get rid of the rat droppings that lay inches thick — something that had never occurred to me but that Dee had foreseen. We spent hours with dustpan and brush cleaning out each little area between the joists. We stood up when the roof space allowed, but otherwise we were on our knees, brushing and shovelling the dirt into rubbish bags. Dee produced the face masks which protected us from inhaling the worst of the dust and smell. Nevertheless, it was one of the most revolting jobs imaginable. At some point she went down to the kitchen and made us a cup of tea which we managed to drink lying amongst the woollen batts, the air so thick with dirt and rat aroma that you knew the tea was layered with them too.

By lunch time we'd finished the worst and Dee somehow coaxed me back down the ladder so that I could wash and enjoy a sandwich in the sunshine. I didn't think I'd ever get up there again but in time I worked out a way of climbing in and out of the roof space which was manageable, if stressful. Laying the batts was simple, the wool nice to handle, and once we had a technique going we worked fast until the area was completely covered. Now an efficient fire warmed the farmhouse and its heat stayed inside rather than escaping through the ceiling. Things were beginning to feel quite snug and we returned to the city filthier than usual, but with the now familiar sense of satisfaction and achievement.

All these hands-on jobs were taxing and you may wonder why a well-paid professional like me, severely short of time, should have bothered to do so many of these tasks around the farm myself. It would have been less trouble to employ others to do the carting or the unskilled jobs like insulation laying. It would have been simpler, safer and less stressful, but this would have defeated the purpose of having the farm. I'd bought it to escape the stresses of life in the city and to reclaim the part of myself that I'd lost through my medical school work. The jobs I did on the house renovation certainly brought their own stresses, but they were of quite a different sort. Constantly challenged by my involvement in the building work, I was forced to learn practical skills and to gain knowledge which I didn't need for my cosseted life in the city.

Besides, living in the country, miles from power or sealed roads required a level of independence and self-reliance. If I was ever to spend much time at the farm I had to understand as much as possible about how it operated; I couldn't call a plumber up every time a tap dripped, I had to know where my water supply was and how to keep it clean, just as I would need to know all about sewage disposal and power generation.

I was starting to realise that one day I would be living there alone — then I'd have to be almost as knowledgeable as Andy about the inner workings of my house. Involvement in the mundane jobs of renovation gave me a sense of confidence and know-how that I could never gain by merely writing cheques for other people to do the work. I was becoming mistress of my own house and edging closer to being mistress of my destiny as well.

A stable changed my life

By late September that year I was in Yokohama attending the International AIDS conference when the dean's secretary tracked me down — he'd finally decided the date for a big public lecture I was to give and it was in three weeks' time. That wasn't much warning for a major presentation so once back from Japan I'd have to devote all my spare time to getting it written. There'd be no rushing over to the farm at weekends, no leisurely lunch hours in the demolition yards — life was going to be pushed for a while. Neither of us knew it then but with this small, slightly inconsiderate act the dean set the wheels in motion for me to escape from his world much sooner than might otherwise have been possible.

Last minute pressures and deadlines were quite common at the medical school but that year I'd found coping with them easier than usual. Owning a farm seemed to have energised rather than tired me, and my lightness of spirit made the difficult work easier and the boring bits bearable. I was looking forward to giving the lecture, even though I'd have liked a bit more time to prepare it!

Back from the conference, I spent the first weekend confined to my study, poring over voluminous books and scribbling rough notes while sun streamed in the windows and birds beckoned me to join them in the garden. My large, rambling house was more than just a home; it was a refuge, a creation, and a part of myself which I'd treasured for many years. But since buying the farm I'd begun to neglect it. I don't mean that it was no longer cared for but, in the way that one can drift out of love, my allegiance had gradually shifted. Somewhere in the depths of my mind I knew that it would not be possible for me to keep both places going — neither financially nor practically — and I knew that one day, far in the future, my new affair with the farm was going to win out.

But none of this was in my head as I enjoyed the spring sun and focused on the challenge of the lecture. It was my Inaugural Professorial Lecture — a tradition in most universities where a new professor has to present an open lecture to the whole faculty. It's an opportunity to show off your knowledge and illustrate why you were appointed — a fairly daunting prospect and one you want to be well prepared for. You can speak on anything you like for as long as you like and I'd chosen to review the state of public health research. Perhaps I felt pushed along by the shortage of time but that afternoon, feeling inspired and confident, my thoughts flowed naturally and I made good progress.

At some point I took a break from the work, made myself a coffee and had a quick glance through the Saturday paper — quite a treat now as I was so rarely in the city on a weekend. Automatically seeking out the Farms for Sale column, I noticed in the Real Estate section of the paper an advertisement for some apartments in the inner city. I'd rented one for a while and knew they were interesting and well located, wedged between the park and downtown area. Previously only available for rent, with the recent death of the owner they were being sold off individually. At the price advertised they seemed amazingly cheap.

I had no intention of buying one, but for old times' sake and perhaps to give myself a break away from the lecture writing, I rang the agent and arranged to view them with him later in the afternoon. His tall, bulky presence and the pervasive smell of his after-shave probably contributed to the feeling of claustrophobia I had on being shown the apartments. They were as attractive as I remembered but much smaller, each having just one large living area and a bedroom. How could my possessions and I ever have fitted into this space? Currently I was filling a two-storeyed house with several bedrooms.

I apologised for wasting his time and explained that they were too small. I tried to get away but the agent mentioned that one apartment was on a double title and came with additional but separate living space. In the mood for further diversion, I let him lead me round the back to a beautiful century-old brick stables. Looking more like a London mews than a Christchurch backstreet, here the loose boxes had been converted to garages, the groom's room into a laundry and the spacious former hay loft had a high vaulted ceiling, wide rimu floorboards and small dormer windows. Shutters and double glass doors covered the hole where the hay had come through. In one corner there was a new kitchen, in another a tiny bathroom nestled, otherwise it was just a big open space. My imagination ran wild. I'd always had dreams of living in one large room — most of us who grew up in the 1960s had such thoughts — and here was my chance. Surely this wonderful space combined with the apartment below would be enough for me to live in, particularly now that I was spending every spare moment at the farm.

Trying hard to hide my feelings from the over-perfumed agent, I went home totally captivated, any ideas of lecture-writing quite abandoned. An hour later I rang the man back and told him I wanted to make an offer and by teatime I'd signed all the papers and unconditionally offered the asking price. I didn't have the money but I was sure I could sell my house and if I had to have a month or two of bridging finance I could cope.

As it turned out I did the right thing to move so quickly since all the apartments were sold by the end of the week, but it was very uncharacteristic of me to behave like this. On impulse, without any consideration of the consequences, I'd catapulted myself into a totally different life — one that meant giving up all the joy of a large house in the leafy suburbs, something I'd strived for years to achieve, and abandoning all the hopes and dreams that went with it. But somehow, as with my decision to buy the farm, I knew my precipitous action was right. Where else could I find such a beautiful space in the centre of a city and with a huge park at its doorstep? More importantly, this new development fitted exactly the escape plan that was beginning to hatch in my mind. I said a silent thank you to my boss for ensuring I was in the city on that precise weekend and without a second thought launched myself into a new sphere of life.

Spring is the time to sell old wooden houses in Christchurch so within a couple of weeks I'd put my beloved home on the market. Feeling heartbroken and disloyal, I stayed well away when potential buyers came through, suffering as if the house was being raped, or at least considered for it. I was surprised that it didn't sell immediately, incredulous when reports came back that the rooms were too big or that the kitchen needed modernising. To me the house was perfect and warranted no criticism.

The big lecture came and went; somehow I'd managed to complete it successfully despite the upheavals in my home life. Now the pace of work began to slow as the academic year ground to its finale and at last I could turn my mind to other matters.

As soon as possible I made my usual end-of-year visit to the accountant, only this time I went with excitement in my heart and anxiety in my stomach. I had a crucial question to put to him and was nervous about his possible response. As chatty as ever, he probably noticed nothing strange, but when the moment came for my question I felt tongue-tied and shy, unsure how to phrase it. I was a young woman in my forties; the word 'retirement' had rarely passed my lips before, and never with respect to myself. I felt embarrassed, as if I were mentioning period pains to an elderly uncle.

In previous visits to my accountant I'd only discussed ways of making money, not ways of giving it up. It felt impolite, almost disrespectful, to raise the subject. Finally I mumbled an innocuous version of my question: How much capital did you need to be able to retire? He had no simple answer but probed for more detail and got a more coherent story from me. I told him I'd traded down, was about to move out of an expensive piece of real estate into a cheap one, and wondered whether I could survive on the money that would be freed up as a result.

I told him I wanted to leave work to go and live on the farm, hoping that it would make some money in the long term, but in the meantime I needed a source of income.

At that moment my future was in my accountant's hands. If he'd laughed at me and dismissed my enquiries as ridiculous I might have taken the idea no further. Always a bit overawed by professionals, I could easily have been made to feel silly or patronised, which might have left me tied to the medical school for decades more. But in fact he gave me a straightforward and factual reply, treating me and my question entirely seriously, and not until we shook hands at the end of the meeting did a smile cross his face.

I probably wouldn't have the amount of money he thought was required but I was jubilant with relief, as if voicing the question and receiving a serious reply confirmed I was on the right path, even if it would take some time to reach the destination.

When the first of December came round — the anniversary of my buying the farm — I spent the evening at home alone, celebrating and looking back on a year of incredible developments. The farm was well along the way to transformation and even more dramatic were the changes it had brought to me. In one brief year I'd left behind the overworked, time-pressured and totally committed academic with vague fantasies of another life; now I had a clear picture of what that life was to be and how to get there. I had abandoned the persona of a socialising, cappuccino-sipping city dweller who'd read all the latest books and seen all the newest films. I had become a bit of a hermit, disinterested in the political news of the day but fascinated by the long-range weather forecast. Not surprisingly, I'd lost a few friends along the way — I was no longer available to meet up with them, and we had fewer interests in common — but my life was infinitely richer and my soul more settled than it had been since I began working 25 years before.

I was due to take over ownership of the apartment in mid-December, but my house had not yet sold so I arranged for a loan with the bank — money was easy to get but interest rates high — so my salary was going to be stretched thin for a while and work on the farmhouse might have to slow down. But for now it continued. Andy had made excellent progress and was sure he'd have it habitable by Christmas, but the next job was the kitchen and I was holding this up because I hadn't found a suitable unit. It had to be of a certain size and shape to fit the space and of the right materials for the feel of the place. Formica and stainless steel combinations from the 1960s would look dreadful as would a 1990s post-modern style, even if I'd been able to afford it. Although I haunted the demolition yards as never before, nothing seemed to come up and I was beginning to despair. When, at the last minute, the solution was revealed, it was so obvious I couldn't imagine why I hadn't seen it before.

My house was still on the market and one evening I was mulling over the latest report from the real estate agent. Apparently a woman had been interested in buying the house but had decided against it. Inadequate access to the back garden meant she would want to put French doors through the scullery which she decided was too big a job.

I looked at the scullery with new eyes. A tiny room, not much more than a passageway off the kitchen, it had a lovely old kauri sink unit and bench top with a hanging storage cupboard above. Why would you want to sacrifice them for a set of doors? Of course, that was when the idea struck. Surely this was the kitchen unit for the farm. I measured it up: precisely the right size, angled in exactly the right way, made of the right materials and of the right era. Taking it out would make no difference to the value of this house and I could redecorate the space so that you'd never know it was gone. Grabbing the phone, I called Andy who cautioned that he would have to come and see whether it could be taken out intact, but a couple of days later he was there and with his usual enthusiasm agreed to give it a try.

The removal job would have to happen quickly and I'd have to repaint and refurnish immediately; with the house on the market I must complete the job in between visits from real estate agents with potential buyers.

Andy and Chris came over on the Saturday, working hard to get the old unit out with minimal damage. By evening they had the trailer and van loaded with a sorry-looking collection of sink unit, bench top and cupboards, leaving me disappointed at the unappealing bits and pieces they'd gathered, and despondent over the plundering and destruction of my beautiful little scullery. But Andy was optimistic. For him the job had gone well with no disasters or unforeseen problems, and he set off back to the peninsula with a cheery wave, agreeing to meet me at the farm the following weekend when the kitchen would be complete.

Now it was my turn to work hard, getting the scullery presentable and the house back to normal as soon as possible. I hired a sander and spent Sunday on my knees cleaning up the floor and putting on coats of polyurethene. Then I painted the walls to cover the big gaps left by the units, and on Monday night when everything was dry, moved in several small pieces of furniture. As if by magic, it looked as good as before, was almost as functional, and when the real estate agent came round next he didn't even notice the change so it obviously wasn't going to detract from the sale.

Now I understood why the house hadn't sold quickly and how fortuitous it was that an unknown woman had criticised its access. The decision to leave that house was one of the saddest of my life, but being able to take away a small piece of it with me, a piece that would become the heart of my farm, was a great comfort.

Andy called me on Wednesday night, bubbling over with excitement. They'd completed the kitchen but he wouldn't tell me anything about it, wanting me to see it for myself. I managed to get out there on Friday afternoon and Andy led me round to the side door. He wanted me to be fully facing the unit for my first glimpse of the kitchen. Immediately I understood his excitement. The unit was perfect. It looked as if it had been there for 100 years with its sink right under the window, the way the two benches fit exactly the spaces available to them and their plain kauri tops blended with the totara of the walls. The heavy cupboard doors matched the solid feel of the house, while the glass-fronted hanging cupboard was of exactly the right proportions and allowed the wooden wall behind to glow through. We couldn't have done better if we'd built it to order!

By the end of that week it was Christmas and, as promised, Andy had got the farm habitable — not what most people would call habitable, but it was warm, dry and had hot and cold water. I got out there on Christmas Eve, just in time for supper and carol-singing around the piano at my friends' farmhouse in the next bay. I met several of my neighbours for the first time and enjoyed their warmth and acceptance, but as darkness approached, I felt like Cinderella, leaving the party despite the early hour and lively atmosphere. With nothing for lighting except candles, I didn't want to make my way home after dark. So by 10 p.m. I was back at the farm and in bed. Well, perhaps 'in bed' is not quite accurate; there was a mattress on the bedroom floor and with Vita curled up beside me, I huddled in a sleeping bag and watched the light fade from the sky, trying not to look at the tatty silver-paper clad and spider web-encrusted walls. But I slept reasonably well and we woke to watch the dawn together as the brilliant red sun rose slowly out of the sea.

It was Christmas Day, I'd had my first night alone on the farm and was to have my first Christmas on the peninsula. Neighbour, Hugh, had invited several of us to breakfast and as I made my way over the hills to his house with Vita dashing about at my side, I felt nothing could be better with the world.

Cloudy by name, cloudy by nature.

The outside bath on the salvaged chimney bricks.

The house begins to look quite civilised. 2000.

Room with a view: the author's studio.

Neighbours celebrate the opening of Hinewai Track in 2002.
From left: the author with Kris Hannon, John Hancock, Hugh Wilson, Fiona Farrell, Paul Newport, Doug Hood, Giles Hancock (obscured) and Hilary Hancock.

Heather and the author with Millie,
Vita and Nisi on the front steps.

Nikau reminder

Banks Peninsula is the southernmost place in New Zealand where nikau palms grow in the wild. At 2000 feet my land was much too high for their survival but apparently you could find clusters of them in areas close to the sea and Hugh had told me that there were one or two in the bay below my farm.

Of all New Zealand's flora and fauna, nikau palms and cabbage trees have a special attraction for me as they do for many who come from the colder regions of Europe. Their form is so entirely foreign to our eyes, their single trunk and fleshy fronds so different from the deciduous oaks and elms of our childhoods. They suggest warm, balmy nights with a promise of exotic smells and sweet juicy fruit. (In reality they offer none of these but somehow the possibilities remain.)

Cabbage trees grow so readily that they have been domesticated and can be found in any suburban garden, pushing ever upwards and depositing dead fronds on neatly mown lawns. Nikau palms, on the other hand, are much rarer, steadfastly retaining their independence from civilization. You can see them on the West Coast, springing up in droves to march across otherwise decimated paddocks, and there are areas of the North Island where they are similarly common, but for most city dwellers, the paintings of Stanley Palmer are about as close as you can get to the real thing.

Hugh's mention of nikau palms growing in my own valley offered a promise of excitement and adventure which had to be satisfied so on Boxing Day, the first day of my first holiday on the farm, I set off to find them.

Two farms link my ridge-line property with the sandy, half-moon bay below, and an unsealed road joins us together, winding slowly down the contours of the hills on the southern side. Entering that valley was a bit like stepping into the frame of a familiar picture. For over a year I'd admired this view of the gentle slopes leading to a wide sweep of sand; it was a constant presence but, so far, I'd never found the time to go down there.

The day dawned warm and cloud-free with only a hint of wind. I stocked my backpack with provisions and started off early while there was no one else around. Following the road relentlessly downhill, Vita and I set quite a pace on the dry, hard surface so that by our first drink stop I was rosy and glowing, the muscles in my thighs beginning to groan. Stopping for the second time, but still only about a quarter of the way down, I began to regret my romantic notion of leaving the car at the farm. But eventually, when we'd almost reached the flat, we got our reward. Rounding a bend that opened up the view we found ourselves suddenly in the presence of a tall, silent guardian standing in the midst of green pasture. In the distance were the outlines of three more.

Despite being a bit wind-battered, these nikau were wonderful specimens. They stood proud and straight, their smooth, narrow trunks about 30 feet high and crowned with bright greenery that was startlingly like a punk hairstyle. They swayed gently in the breeze and their fronds rustled enticingly. I was struck by their placid air — they stood unaffected by the changes to the landscape they'd witnessed over the years, seeming oblivious to their lack of companions and content merely to watch over the land and wait for the day when their whanau would return.

I sat by the roadside and ate my sandwiches as I looked across at them. Vita found a few inches of shade and fell deeply asleep, able to give up her role as guard to these green gods. There is something very spiritual about nikau. Their form hints at regality and higher purpose. Sitting in their presence I felt refreshed and comforted with the same sense of peace that accompanies a spell inside the dim interior of an Italian church. Yet despite this calmness of spirit there was something about the scene that disturbed me; there was an air of divinity but also of isolation. Why were there only four nikau when there could have been four hundred?

They were a stark reminder of the devastation we have brought to our land. Here on the valley floor were lush green meadows mimicking the best of English countryside and on the hills above stretched bare grasslands now browning in the summer heat, their surface pitted with scars and slips where heavy rain had taken great clumps of topsoil off down the hill. Only the odd shrub or tree interrupted the vast expanse of pasture. The process of burning and clearing the natural bush cover and seeding it in grass had been repeated all over New Zealand. It had meant economic prosperity for millions but I wondered at what cost to the earth?

After mulling over these thoughts for an hour or so I roused Vita from her dreams and began the long trek home, enjoying the view up the valley as it slowly unfolded. There were signs of bush regeneration in the gullies and I passed a few areas of beautiful native trees, but the loneliness of the nikau sentries stayed with me. They reminded me of my purpose in buying the farm — not to save an old house, nor to find a new life, but rather in some tiny way to contribute to the recovery of the original vegetation.

In the year since I'd bought the farm so much of my time and attention had been given to the house that I had hardly given a thought to the bush. Yet it was ever-present, like the backdrop of a painting in which the house provided the foreground interest. The house was nothing without its dramatic views and majestic landscape. The experience with the nikau helped me get that back in proportion.

I wandered slowly on, climbing the hill at a pace that my body and the heat of the day allowed, and was more than halfway back up the valley when a glinting near the tops caught my eye. With a smack of recognition I realised it was my own roof catching the sun's rays and sending them back to me. I'd never seen the house or farm from this angle, never considered what impact I might be having on my neighbours' views. At first I was entranced — there was my little house tucked up under the hillside, nestled into its leafy surrounds. This could be the cover painting for a book of ancient fairytales, like every child's dream of where goblins or elves might live. But then I saw it differently. From here the house was a mere dot on a contour, surrounded by that sea of green and flanked by tall totara, while the size of the peaks behind reminded me of the insignificance of what I was doing. If I stopped restoration tomorrow the house would soon melt into the earth — the elements and the vegetation would take it back into themselves. I'd spent a full year of my life making a small impact on this house, yet the growth of the bush and the landscape itself were much greater. This strangely comforting thought reminded me that the bush regenerated of its own accord. If I could be a benevolent guardian, keeping it free of browsing animals, then in time the bush would recover, much faster than if I tried to interfere.

I got back to the farm well before dark, but it had been a long, hot day. My body was slowing down to match the rhythm of the land. My anxieties, so pressing before Christmas, were fading to a blur, the parts of me I lost in the hurly-burly of work, gradually re-awakening. This was what had driven me to the country in the first place and, after only a short stay, it was surprising how quickly I began to feel restored.

The next day was dull and overcast. The birds sang on but the sun never got through the thick cloud cover. I kept the log-burner going all day and spent much of it lying around with Vita, resting overworked muscles, enjoying the warmth of the house and forgetting that it was still derelict and bare inside. I soaked in a long, hot bath with the window wide open so that I could almost believe I was out there in the bush. Periodically the sounds and smells swept over me and once a black and white tomtit perched on the window ledge, peering in at this strange apparition.

Later, sitting up at the trestle by the window, I drank red wine and watched the colours change on the sea. Somewhere out of sight the sun was setting, a drama reflected on the hills, ocean and sky as pinks and yellows changed quickly to deep red and orange then faded completely. I marvelled again at this piece of isolated paradise. Only the lights of fishing boats on the horizon, and the hum of an occasional car passing my gate gave any clue that others were in the world.

As each day passed on the farm I became more aware of the life that did inhabit the place. The tomtit was the closest anything came to the house, but in the trees the bellbirds sang constantly to each other with a variety of calls that would make even Kiri Te Kanawa jealous. Occasionally a native wood pigeon swooped by — disturbing Vita in her sleep and scaring me with its sudden heavy presence, and one night I was woken by a strange noise — the echoing cry of a morepork, but I soon slept again, lulled by its repetitive call. I became quieter and calmer and could now sit still on a rocky outcrop to glimpse a flash of vivid green gecko or catch the whisper of a field mouse looking for seed in the tall grass.

Before I knew it my holiday was over, but after a week of sleeping on a hard floor, eating very simple meals and talking only to the dog, I was ready to return to Christchurch and my other life.

Work began again in the gradual way it does after the Christmas break when half the population still seems to be lying on a beach somewhere and the other half wish they were too. It left me plenty of time to think about the farm and how to begin the inside renovation now that most of the construction work was complete. At least in this area I had a bit more knowledge and confidence. Having painted numerous flats and houses and once even worked as a contract painter, I thought of myself as a bit of an interior designer and had a couple of suburban makeovers to my credit. But the challenge of decorating a derelict farmhouse was going to stretch any skills I might have acquired in the past.

The walls inside the house were made from narrow strips of totara in what was called 'match lining'. Years ago this would have been covered with scrim, a heavy-duty hessian, with wall-paper pasted onto that. But all this had disintegrated long ago except where pieces of scrim hung off old nails or around the very tops of the walls where there was a vague pattern on a border paper. Now the walls were covered with a silver foil insulating material stapled straight onto the boards, which previous owners had put up to keep the house warm during their occasional visits. Maybe it fulfilled that purpose but it was ugly, dirty and a breeding ground for insects of all descriptions.

I wanted to strip off all the foil and expose the beautiful totara boards but this would let all the draughts in and probably reduce the temperature considerably. A compromise was called for. By stripping all the internal walls to their bare wood I could get the visual effect I wanted, while those which backed onto the outside of the house could be left in their foil wrapping and covered with plaster board to give protection from the cold.

Off I went to the building suppliers and got the trailer loaded with large sheets of gib-board, praying it wouldn't rain before I got to the farm where Andy waited to help me unload. A few days later he began putting up the board in the main living area.

By my next visit he'd finished lining the three external walls to make the room white, bright and clean, which left the one still covered with sheets of silver foil looking worse than ever. A couple of friends had come to the farm with me and we all set to with vigour to remove the foil from this wall, not giving a thought to the possible consequences.

Gin and Rosie, owners of a café in Christchurch, are the sort of unflappable people who can handle twenty orders in five minutes and still have time to chat to the customers. They take everything in their stride, so clambering on chairs or boxes and pulling off chunks of silver foil was nothing to them. But unknown to me, Gin has a terror of moths, some incident as a child having left her with a phobia of silent flying creatures. So it was quite a disaster when one of the pieces of foil she pulled off disturbed a collection of large brown moths from their daylight slumbers. They flew blindly about, knocking against windows and people indiscriminately. Soon the room resembled a scene from a horror movie as Gin tried desperately to get rid of the moth lodged in her bushy hair. After that she resorted to huddling in the rain outside until we'd got the wall completely clear of its moth covering and it was safe to come back in.

At last calm returned and we drank strong coffees to recover while contemplating the wooden wall now revealed in its virginal state — probably something the original builder would never have intended. It wasn't finished or planed; the simple rough-hewn boards were freckled with nail holes where scrim or picture hooks had been attached. Saw marks on the wood showed they'd been crafted by hand, not by machine, which gave each a slight variation in width and thickness.

Even in this unfinished state there was beauty in the contrast between the smooth white of the plastered walls and the rough warm glow of the bare one. It was the wooden one that drew your attention even if the plastered ones looked so clean by comparison.

Now of course I was impatient to begin painting these newly lined walls but lecturing had started up again and it was difficult to get much time away. And then there was another problem: I discovered you can't just paint gib-board; it has to be 'stopped' first, which means plastering all the joints between boards and in corners to make one smooth and continuous surface. Dee offered to do this and I was grateful, but I had no idea how difficult it was, nor how obsessional she could be. Weeks went by before she was satisfied enough with her job to let me start the painting. She is a perfectionist whereas I am a pragmatist which proved a dreadful combination as I agitated to get going and she cautioned that the finish wasn't quite good enough yet and needed one more tidy up.

Finally the weekend came when I took ladders and rollers and started painting the living area. Beginning with several coats of flat white to give lightness and brightness, I finished by rag-rubbing with a dip of yellow to add a sense of antiquity in keeping with the age of the building. The season was turning to autumn but it was warm enough that the paint dried quickly, so it only took about three weekends to get it complete. The finished effect was just what I wanted — a clean, light living space. I had no curtains and very little furniture but, for the first time, I felt this old building was becoming a home.

The painting was the first renovation I'd been able to do on my own, my contribution until now being simply to help Andy or Dee as glorified apprentice. With the decorating I came into my own and began to gain a sense of creativity and satisfaction as the inside slowly changed.

With water and heating the house had become a much

nicer place to work; a kettle was always on the boil and a hot bath ready to follow a Saturday of hard labour. I still had to go to bed soon after dark because candles and kerosene lamps were the only source of lighting, and bed was still a mattress on the floor in an unlined room, but things were definitely improving.

But now I had to concentrate all spare energy and time on my life in the city. I'd finally sold the big house and faced moving out of it into the apartment. Twelve years' worth of accumulated possessions, junk and memorabilia needed to be sorted quite carefully so that nothing got thrown out that I'd later regret. Beginning the job conservatively, by the end I became quite ruthless and finally had things down to a manageable level. Someone lent me space in their garage to store things I hoped to take out to the farm and I crammed the apartment and its garage full. When the day came to hand over the keys to my house it was as if my whole life had been reduced down and put in packing cases. I'd spent years building up this home; it was unsettling how quickly and easily it could be destroyed. But this was an inevitable step in the transformation of my life, ill-defined though its course might be, and somehow that kept my spirits up. Also, once settled into the apartment, I began to enjoy being in the central city — the pleasure of walking through the park to work, of wandering down for a coffee on Saturday morning and of never having to search for a car park when going out at night.

The reluctant traveller

One of the perks of life as an academic is study leave — a chance to spend a term or two at another university where you have little teaching but plenty of time for research and reflection. As you can imagine, it's a great treat and something to look forward to for years. So it was odd that now, when the chance came to have three months' leave in Europe, I didn't want to take it. This was all the fault of the farm — I hated to think of missing even one week without a visit there, let alone three months.

But arrangements of this sort are made well in advance and not easily undone so in the middle of June, 1996, just as winter began, I had to leave. Dee promised to keep an eye on everything for me. She offered to lag the pipes so that they didn't freeze or crack in the cold weather, and Andy said he'd carry on with the building by putting on the wooden verandah. This was to go along three sides of the house, leaving only the colder, southerly side bare, and was to be wide enough to take a large-sized table for outside meals, and plenty of seats. We'd put piles in for the verandah when the house was being re-piled, but I'd delayed on the construction until the inside of the house was more complete and my money supply allowed. Now Andy said it would be done by the time I returned.

Tree planting was another thing to organise. If I were to put in more Douglas firs then winter was the time to do it. Most of the seedlings already in had survived and put on growth. Those in the more exposed areas struggled a bit, but the majority were alive and well. I asked the forestry contractor to finish planting the paddock he'd begun last year.

Just before leaving I made one final visit to the farm with a good friend, Janine, who was down from Wellington. It was early winter but the snow had already come. Parking as close as we safely could, we walked down the road to the gate, clutching sticks of French bread for lunch and marvelling at the light. Sun glistened on the snow, the sky was a tropical blue, and the silence palpable. I had that sense of passing into a different world.

Janine is a bit of a food buff and within minutes she had a table set in the snow with a scrumptious array of cheeses and pesto. The sun was warm and the glare so bright it forced us to don sunglasses with our woolly hats. Vita sat peacefully at our sides, grateful for the odd taste of camembert and happy to be back in her snowy kingdom again. Above us an occasional bird sang out; its ringing call clearer than ever over the muffled landscape.

I couldn't bear the thought of leaving all this for dirty, noisy, over-peopled Europe and during lunch began to complain about having to go. Janine soon brought me back to my senses. A great traveller, she's spent many years living around the Pacific, sometimes in quite dangerous places. She gave me a good telling-off for being so unadventurous and unappreciative. Friends like this can be very helpful!

I took a suitcase crammed with photos, determined not to

forget the farm and its isolation even when surrounded by the materialistic attractions of Europe. To many of my colleagues there I must have seemed like someone from another planet. These were people I'd met during my postgraduate studies in England, or academics I knew from international conferences. On previous visits I'd been just like them: taken up with university politics; oppressed by the workload; fascinated by developments in our discipline, but now we had little in common. While I waxed lyrical about the smells of the bush they talked about their newest shopping complex; I bemoaned the problems of gorse control while they complained about car parking and the struggle of getting to and from work. The photos helped them understand a little of my new self — they loved the sunshine, clear sky and lack of traffic — but few of them could imagine a life without electricity and the gadgets that dominated their days.

In between conferences and other commitments I spent time with my sister in England. Practical yet sophisticated, she shares my love of doing up houses but not of the rural life. She was intrigued by the challenges the farm offered, but horrified at the thought of actually living there. She could admire the views in my photos but her eyes glazed over as I raved on about the desolate beauty of the land. Keen to help with the restoration, she took me to stores where you could find interior decorating items for any building style imaginable. She led me down back alleys to an obscure shop in Leeds where, at a price I could afford, we bought metres and metres of heavy blue linen to make the curtains for the living area.

It had been churlish of me not to want to go to Europe. I had a thoroughly stimulating time visiting several universities and catching up with friends and family whom I'd begun to neglect since buying the farm. More importantly, the time away gave me a chance to reflect on life, to take stock and get some perspective on where I was going. I'd become obsessed with the farm and it did me good to get away from it. There were no regrets, only great joy at the pleasure it had given me, but it had become a much larger project than anticipated. I'd started the venture with no real idea of its purpose, but now it was becoming clearer. The farm was no longer a little hobby, a distraction from work; it was becoming my life.

From twelve thousand miles away, I schemed about my future and how to stop work and live on the farm full-time. I couldn't leave work immediately — there were still large expenses to cover like getting power, a phone and a toilet on the place, and by the time my income stopped I wanted the farmhouse to be completely habitable. But things were definitely moving towards that point. Now that I'd sold the house I was mortgage-free and this was surely the first step in becoming income-free.

There was also the possibility of superannuation. When I turned 50 next year, I'd be eligible for a payment — tiny, since I'd only been contributing to the scheme for a short time, but a regular monthly income even so. Perhaps I could live very cheaply on the farm, renting out the apartment in town to provide for its ongoing costs, and the capital left from the house sale would earn some income and provide an emergency fund. With hope in my heart and this idea crystallising in my mind, I started the journey back to New Zealand.

By September when I got home, winter was past its peak, but I had lots of work to catch up on so several weekends went by before I got out to the farm. By then the snow had melted, leaving flattened grasses on the hillsides but scattered amongst them the shrubs and young natives pushed upwards more strongly than ever. The tall trees looked refreshed by their dowsing in winter rains and the fuchsia branches, naked from a distance, on closer inspection revealed perky new growth. Heaving a sigh of relief, I felt the cold fresh air invigorate me deep inside. The time away had been relaxing and restorative but it was so good to be back.

Down at the house I was welcomed by a big, new verandah which gave a sense of separation from the bush and almost doubled the floor space. It was a transition zone between inside and out and offered unparalleled views and lots of sitting spots. Putting the verandah on three sides of the house had been a good decision — there would always be some shade and some full sun, one sheltered side and one breezy. Andy had done a great job, as promised, with the macrocarpa boards already taking on a grey and aged tinge that would soon blend well with the ancient totara of the house.

Warming my hands on a mug of tea, I sat by the window feeling very pleased — I'd left the farm on its own for three months and returned to find it in a better state than ever, no wash-outs with the rain nor plumbing problems with the snow. I walked off down the farm track to inspect the new trees, feeling like a colonial tea planter surveying his holdings in Ceylon after a spell 'at home'. But my smug satisfaction was soon shattered.

As far as the eye could see were neat rows of newly planted seedlings looking healthy and happy, each surrounded by a circle of 'weed release' where spray had killed the competing vegetation. Everything appeared exactly as I'd hoped — except they were all planted in the wrong place.

The new Douglas firs should have been put in the paddock furthest from the house but they'd been planted in the one designated for native regeneration, an area covenanted for this purpose and one I was legally obliged to keep free of other species. I couldn't imagine how the forestry consultant had misunderstood which paddock he was to plant. With thousands of trees now growing illegally, I was both furious and worried. I crossed from one side of the paddock to the other but there was no escape from the facts. Over its length and breadth little green sticks poked from the ground in rows like elite troops on parade.

With the light fading I had to leave for the city but driving back I felt frustrated and powerless, almost the same way I'd felt in the early days when the gorse problem had overwhelmed me. What happened when these battalions of trees started coming up through the native bush?

However, I calmed down after speaking to the consultant. Apparently there had been a thick fog the day of the planting; it seemed the workers had become disorientated and had strayed by mistake across the fence-line. He assured me they'd remove all the errant seedlings and replant them where they should be. I was relieved, but it was a good lesson for me. I'd possibly been too lackadaisical in my instructions; a 'real' farmer would never have been so casual as to make such arrangements on the phone. I should have walked the land with the consultant and confirmed where the trees were to go.

In time he put it all right and the seedlings survived their uprooting and relocation at such a tender age. The odd one was missed and now the occasional foreign head appears amongst the natives. But this proves a bonus each December when I set out with a handsaw and return with a prize Christmas tree, feeling virtuous for removing a 'weed'.

Having settled back into work after the time away, I spent all my spare nights and weekends making up the curtains with the material I'd bought in England. Already thick and heavy, when lined with a thermal backing, each curtain seemed to weigh a ton. The full length, double pairs for the French doors were especially weighty. They were going to need substantial hanging rods and a local blacksmith came to the rescue. He visited the farm to get the feel of the place then created simple but ingenious iron rods that turned back on themselves to make for easy attachment to the wall. Their simple design was well matched to the solid, unadorned house.

When all was ready I went over to put up the curtains, which almost broke my arms. But the result was great; their deep colour and texture gave warmth and created a sense of security. Now at night I was hidden from the outside — I'd felt vulnerable exposed to any eyes out there, even if they were only possums' or rabbits' eyes — but with curtains drawn and log-burner roaring, my formerly freezing, rat-infested room was a warm, private retreat.

The next challenge was doing up the floors. As it turned out, this process brought an unexpected reward. Cheaper and more profound than a course of psychotherapy, the job gave me sudden insight into my behaviour which surprised as much as it comforted.

Fitted carpet wasn't a sensible option for this house — it would be warm but impossible to keep clean with no electricity for a vacuum cleaner — so bare wooden floors and thick rugs seemed the solution. In an earlier life the matai floorboards would have been varnished and polished, but now after years of neglect and dirt they were a dark brown grunge colour.

Without power I couldn't use a floor sander but found the formula for a Condy's crystals solution which would take off the remains of the varnish. A long-time friend and professional cleaner, Bon, came out to help me and we spent the day in prayer position, rubbing on the formula, scrubbing off coats of varnish and mopping up the resultant dirt. It was hard work but rewarding. With her greatly superior skills, Bon did most of the job but my aching joints gave me a sense of achievement too.

At the end of the day the floor was a warm golden colour, with a complicated pattern of marks, stains and nicks. After Bon had gone I sat by the fire with a glass of wine, savouring its beauty and contemplating these 'signs'. Just as a geologist can tell the history of a land by its soils so I could read something of my house's history in its floor. The front room boards were in almost perfect condition; it must have been kept for guests and rarely used. Under a south-facing window there was a patch of new flooring where rain had come through a broken pane and rotted the old boards. Where the coal range had been, notches in the wood showed that someone chopping kindling on the hearth had occasionally missed. A hole in the kitchen floor had a matching hole in the ceiling above it. Then my time here had already made its imprint; where I'd removed the old chimney-breast and fireplace was an unsightly patch of concrete.

I wasn't proud of my contribution, but it appealed to my

rootless self to be adding my own marks to the ongoing history of this house. I was surprised at how strongly I felt about that; it was as if stripping away the old layers on the floor had also revealed something in me. Perhaps I'd never faced how alone and stateless I felt; my childhood had been divided between England and Australia. I'd always thought of that travel as an asset, which gave me confidence in both cultures and let me pick out the best of each. But there was a downside: it had left me with a sense that I belonged to neither, so as an adult I'd chosen to live in a different country again. Also, my family had never owned a home.

My father was a vicar so we lived in beautiful rectories, but they were holding pens or bus stops, not permanent homes. That gypsy-like existence gave me a degree of flexibility for which I'd always been grateful, but it had a price; I yearned to put down roots: to have stability and continuity. Now this farm, the bush and the uninterrupted silence of the land were giving me these. By integrating my history with theirs I could at last glimpse a future where I might belong, might gain a sense of purpose, where, in a way, my adult life might begin.

While still vague, this insight made some sense of my recent actions. I'd made some radical changes in my life but the reasons hadn't been obvious to me, let alone to the outside world. I was still performing well at the medical school, but unbeknown to my bosses I was no longer committed to them nor to my academic life. I'd done well in their world, worked hard for approval and success; now I longed to give it all away for a life of simplicity — one where honesty and commitment counted in a way they no longer did in the commercialised university system.

As Christmas approached, and with it the new year, I knew it would soon be time for action.

Cloud Farm is born

Dee's birthday falls in late spring and that year I took her out to the farm for a celebratory picnic. Early in the day I crammed champagne into a backpack with some exotic tartlets from a local delicatessen, picked up Dee and drove over with only one brief stop for coffee on the way. At the farm we scrambled to the highest point and laid out our luxurious feast amongst the tussocks and rocks. Despite the dull day and brisk wind we persevered, sheltering behind the young totara on the tops, toasting the birthday and the view, trying to pretend we were having a great time. Dee hates the cold. Her thin-blooded body is more suited to the northern beaches of Queensland than to the cool coasts of the South Island, so before too long she began to complain. I produced a thermos and tried to distract her with a mug of strong tea, which dulled both the glamour of the occasion and the effects of the champagne!

For some time I'd been trying to find a name for the farm. The only one so far was 'The Saddle', acknowledging an old pack saddle I'd found in the bush, as well as the form the land took, straddling the hill, but the name had never stuck. I hadn't found myself saying, 'I'm going out to "The Saddle"', and people didn't ask about 'The Saddle'. Everyone, including me, still referred to it as 'The Farm'.

As we sat looking over the bay I asked Dee if she had any suggestions and, huddling against the wind, we tossed a few ideas around but nothing appealed. Suddenly the weather closed right in and low cloud obliterated the view, forcing us to give up on the picnic and return to the warmth of the house. Packing up the goodies, Dee said grumpily, 'I think you should call it "Cloud Farm"' and with that she trudged off into the thick fog that now enveloped the picnic site.

So 'Cloud Farm' it became. Now, years later, as I sit at my desk, with clouds swirling around the house, I wonder that such a perfect epithet took so long to present itself. Some days I feel like a 747 pilot looking down over endless and impenetrable froth. On others the farm is totally immersed and you can't see past the edge of the first garden. After several days of that I get cabin fever and have to go down to Akaroa to remind myself that civilisation still exists out there. Just occasionally there are cloud-free days when power surges into the solar panels and it's too hot for the simplest job. Then I live on the verandah, reading books and moving chairs every three hours to follow the shade and the breeze. But more often than not, cloud will have arrived again by nightfall, in wisps across the moon or blurring the horizon between sea and sky. Cloud is more prevalent in summer than in winter. A day can dawn magnificently with the pink sun highlighting a huge cloud bank out at sea. By breakfast that bank will be moving slowly but relentlessly onshore and up the valley until we are engulfed. It will leave again before dusk, lifting so suddenly you wonder if it's really been there and making you appreciate the view more than ever.

Cloud invasions like that are more common around Christmas, and my second at Cloud Farm was particularly bad. By then I had three rooms of the house habitable, some of my furniture moved out of storage and the living area almost comfortable and functioning well. I was able to invite visitors. My cousin Anne from Canada, whom I'd not met before, was the first to arrive. As she stepped off the bus, we recognised each other instantly, drawing on some mysterious genetic knowledge. Together we strung up the Christmas decorations and exchanged stories; her visit made this my first family Christmas in New Zealand since I moved here twenty years before. Somehow it seemed fitting that it should happen at Cloud Farm.

Other friends came later and camped on the few flat spots near the house until we began to resemble a hippy commune. On Christmas morning Hugh arrived for breakfast with his house-load of guests. Our large boisterous group crowded into the house since it was too cool on the verandah. While I cooked scrambled eggs, Anne produced an endless stream of pancakes with real maple syrup she'd carried all the way from Canada.

I'd brought my cat Nisi to the farm for the first time and was worried about her coping with the crowds, but she took everything in her stride, trying out various knees before settling on Hugh's. Vita was in her element; she stared longingly as forks moved from plates to mouths and was there to help at once when toast or egg fell to the floor.

The house was transformed from its normal solid and silent state to one of buzz and clatter; bodies were perched on every surface. The international flavour of the meal matched the guests; one worked for a big charity in Amsterdam, another was about to leave for a job in the restructuring of South

Africa, but all were on the same wavelength despite pursuing different lives in different parts of the world. It was the end of 1996, human rights were being restored in Africa and Eastern Europe. We were optimistic and committed to the future — a feeling the farm seemed to reflect back to us in the glow of its wooden floors and the warmth of its roaring log-burner.

By evening there was another group of visitors eating around the table on the verandah, toasting each other's plans and watching the sky slowly change colour.

These were the first parties the house had seen for decades and it rose to the occasion, but I got the feeling it preferred solitude. Somehow the setting with its grave and gracious totara and the solemn headlands seemed to favour serious, contemplative pursuits over laughter and trivial exchanges. Again I felt the history of the place imposing itself upon me. Life here had been hard; there'd been joy and happiness but not the sort that is achieved through socialising or light-hearted gossip. Fulfilment had come from within, from self-sufficiency and pride in achievement. It seemed crazy to attribute these qualities to a house — if I was starting to anthropomorphise it perhaps I was losing the plot — but it seemed to emanate contentment and peace. I'd felt them on my first day and they'd grown stronger as the house itself had; I must be careful not to abuse them.

After the holiday period, when others started to go home, Anne and I spent the days walking on Hugh's property next door. He'd first begun making the Hinewai Reserve with a small piece of land bought in the 1980s but had managed to add to it over the years so now it stretched almost from sea level to the ridge top and covered a whole valley. The variety of vegetation, bird life and landform was astonishing — particularly to Anne who was used to the huge open spaces of Canada where similar landscapes and habitats run for hundreds of miles. But here, in a mere four mile stretch the land changed from the semi-tropics of sea level to subalpine terrain on the ridges.

Laced with tracks, the reserve offers easy access to its most isolated spots and notable features. It has waterfalls and forest glades, rocky outcrops and gentle flats; you can take serious climbs or easy ambles, plan a walk lasting a whole day or for just half an hour.

Until this holiday with Anne, although I'd visited Hugh often, I'd never found time to fully explore Hinewai. Now, walking all over it, I was full of admiration for him and his work, and thankful again that Cloud Farm was so close to this special piece of New Zealand.

The Ellangowan reserve on my northern boundary is a smaller area of land managed by the Department of Conservation. Featuring magnificent totara forests in the gullies and snow tussocks on the high stony tops, it links up with other tracks which let Anne and I tramp from the farm gate to the sea without setting foot on the road.

Spending these days getting to know the neighbouring countryside made me appreciate how lucky I'd been to find this piece of land surrounded by reserves and walking tracks when it might have been next to farmland and bare paddocks. Instead of silent bush and bellbird song there could have been barking dogs and bleating sheep. It also made me realise the importance of Cloud Farm from an ecological perspective. Wedged between two reserves, the land acted as a corridor between them, encouraging plants, birds and insect life to spread, further consolidating their survival.

We stayed on the farm ten days and I began to appreciate what it might be like to live there all the time. Anne enjoyed her visit and wasn't perturbed by the primitive conditions — she had her own cabin in rural Ontario and knew about life far from civilisation — but the cloudy days were an unpleasant surprise. She was used to summer being summer and winter winter; our weather with its characteristic 'four seasons in one day' took her some time to appreciate!

By New Year's Eve she'd gone off to see more of the South Island and I'd returned to Christchurch for celebrations with my usual friends. Buoyant and optimistic as we were, our resolutions that year seemed more dramatic than normal, full of schemes and promises to start life afresh. Spurred on by the alcohol, I was brave enough to speak openly for the first time about my plans to leave work, but no one took me seriously. Speculating about buying farmhouses in Tuscany, or apartments in Paris, we'd often shared dreams of escape, but few of us had acted on them. One friend had given up a secure job to teach English around the world and another left paid work to set up her own business; both were now happier and more fulfilled as a result. But these were the exceptions. Most of us complained about our work and did nothing about it. Ironically, now that I was intent on change and wanted to gauge my friends' reactions, they didn't believe me. I didn't try to convince them. Lacking confidence about my plans, I accepted their scepticism and resolved not to say more until I was certain of myself and where I was going.

In the after-glow of the celebrations, I took the chance to

think through the consequences of giving up my job. I knew there would be difficulties and not only the practical ones I'd face without an income. What about the psychological impacts of being out of the workforce?

Work had never played a large part in my emotional life; it took many hours of the day but little of my soul. Leaving work would mean giving up a title, some status and a position of power, but these were things that mattered to the outside world and not to me inside. I'd be just the same person without these privileges.

Or was I fooling myself? Without work would I feel like 'a worthless old spinster' as one of my friends feared she might? If I wasn't contributing to the economic well-being of the nation, would I feel like a 'bludger', as another, more politically committed one, felt she would? I didn't think so. I knew paid work wasn't the only way to give back to society and I wasn't going to vegetate or waste my talents. Surely my self-esteem was robust enough to cope with a few criticisms of the 'bludger' sort?

Thinking back to my parents, I felt grateful for the example they'd set, never relying on paid work for a sense of identity. My mother was professionally qualified — quite unusual for women of her era — but work came second to her other interests and activities; it was an adjunct to life, never its main substance.

For many of my friends this was not the case. For them giving up work would seem like losing themselves and their identity. For others there were practical considerations: children, mortgages, or lifestyles made them dependent on regular incomes and unable to seriously contemplate change.

Thinking through these issues, I found none of them applied to me. There were no barriers to me making the changes I wanted.

In Nelson for a week's holiday, I spent the time lying in the sun, planning the year ahead. The drive up through Lewis Pass had been particularly inspiring; it has none of the grandeur of the Haast nor the drama of Arthur's Pass, but it offers more promise than either. Perhaps because the changes unfold so slowly there is more time for contemplation of what lies ahead. As I drove relentlessly north, the rolling hill country turned to high-sided river flats and my heart lifted in anticipation of the challenges and excitements I faced.

In the year ahead I would turn 50 and be eligible to take out superannuation. The work still required at the farm would need one more year's salary, but it would be my last. I had to give at least six months' notice so I'd tell my bosses about my intentions as early as possible. But for now I would keep the decision to myself. I didn't want rumours to unsettle my colleagues nor for my bosses to hear about it from a third party.

Although I felt anxious about my decision, scared about the process of retiring and what people would think, there was also a degree of calm. I was clear and confident that it was the right thing to do, instinctively sure I was following a path that was meant to be.

Back at work, the sense of impending change both unsettled and energised me, but I had plenty to do, finalising several pieces of research before the year was out and installing some key facilities so that Cloud Farm would be ready to become my home.

Solar power comes to Cloud Farm

It may seem contradictory that within weeks of naming my property 'Cloud Farm', I decided to install a power system that relied entirely on the sun for its operation. At the time, the apparent irony passed me by, blinded as I was by the confidence with which I was pursuing life, but I've never regretted the decision to use solar power, despite an occasional worry over battery levels in winter.

Why the house had never been connected to the mains supply is a mystery. There's power to the bay below and to the valleys on either side, but this little pocket of land was left out of the network. Perhaps by the time electricity came to the area the house was already becoming derelict and thought to be past permanent habitation.

So getting power to the property was the first job to do that year and I began with a quote from the local electricity supplier. Their figure of $45,000, although cushioned with justifications, was so prohibitive I could only laugh — even the man who gave it to me was embarrassed — but it forced me to explore other ways of generating power, which turned out to be a good thing.

For Christmas Dee had given me a book on the use of solar power and alternative energy in New Zealand. Here, along with detailed technical guidelines, were examples of households depending entirely on the sun for their power, not only in the tropical north, but as far south as Dunedin. Poring over this book, I tried to grasp how life worked in a solar powered house and, with more difficulty, to understand the components of such a system and how they fit together. Solar wasn't the only possibility; at 2000 feet above the Pacific, Cloud Farm had plenty of wind which might be used for generating power and there were also streams for possible hydro systems.

After reading through the book several times I felt I had a smattering of knowledge but needed expert advice to fully understand it. The Yellow Pages led me to Stuart, an alternative energy specialist living in a suburb of Nelson — sun capital of New Zealand!

Arriving at his home in a new subdivision, I was directed to a monstrous garage underneath the house. The cool, voluminous space was crammed with strange pieces of equipment, huge batteries lining one wall, connectors hanging from hooks on another, and large, flat cardboard boxes holding brilliant blue solar panels stacked on the floor. For three hours Stuart patiently explained the advantages and disadvantages of possible systems and how they worked. Solar panels collected the power, batteries stored it and an inverter adapted the 12 volts of battery power to the 230 volts required for most electrical goods. With less sun in winter you needed other options for charging the batteries. He thought it would be too gusty at my site for wind power and the water flows too small for a hydro system, so a generator would probably be the answer.

Stuart advised on items I needed but recommended I buy them from someone closer to home. He gave me the name of a local supplier. I left with a shopping list of requirements and a much better appreciation of what was involved. I'd taken up his entire morning and he'd gained nothing from it except another convert to the potential of alternative power.

It was going to cost quite a bit to set the system up, but nothing approaching $45,000, and once it was operating, I'd have power for free — no monthly bills or supply charges — which fitted ideally with my intended income-free future.

But first I had to get the house wired with all the paraphernalia that goes with electricity: light fittings, switches, fuse boxes and connectors. Joe, an electrician friend from Christchurch, agreed to do this job; he'd heard about Cloud Farm from mutual friends and was interested to visit. I'd decided on only seven lights and two outlets — it wasn't going to be a power-hungry house — and I could add to them later if required. With no experience of solar power, Joe encouraged this parsimonious attitude, his good Scottish background inclining him to caution.

Joe said the job would be as easy as wiring up a brand new house. He arrived early and beavered away, much of the time bent double in the roof space, an area now warmed by the log-burner below but still smelling of its ratty past. By the end of the day there were light cords hanging from ceilings, switches by doors and power points at strategic places.

Sitting with a wine after Joe had gone, I studied these new protuberances, suddenly conscious of items which normally went unnoticed. In this house from pre-electricity days, they stood out like exemplars of a strange civilisation. I'd become used to uninterrupted ceiling lines, and plastic was hitherto unknown here. Such symbols of modernity clashed with the timeless nature of the house. For a moment I panicked, wondering if connecting the power was a terrible mistake. There was a sense of invasion, of shattered peace, but this was tempered by the excitement of the new. So far these fixtures were impotent decorations; they offered no function of their own, but promised progress and independence from the elements. I thought of my grandmother when her house was connected to power — how strange and exciting for someone who'd known nothing of life with electricity. Reassured and quickly recovering from my panic, I felt the familiar satisfaction as with every step in the renovation I moved faster towards my goal.

Putting in the solar power system was next on the list so once my money had built up after the wiring job, I ordered the equipment and met Joe and Andy at the farm. Andy got up on the roof with his compass to attach the solar panel at its optimum aspect to the sun while Joe wired everything up and I played assistant, making cups of tea when required and dashing off to Akaroa for unanticipated requirements — like stainless steel washers.

By lunchtime we had power. In broad daylight nothing seemed different, but when darkness fell, long after everyone had gone, I experienced the sheer excitement of creating light with the touch of a switch. I'd enjoyed the romantic glow of candles and the ritual lighting of the tilly lamp as the sun set, but the night had closed in on me with only pools of light in the house. Now I felt released from the restrictions of the dark, able to wander from room to room as I chose, to get wood from the shed without shielding a candle from the wind and to read or to write letters after dark. Even more importantly, being able to see into all corners of the house gave me a new and quite irrational sense of security. In the following weeks, when I could get out to the farm, I found my life expanding to fill the new spaces that light offered. I could reward myself after a day of hard work with not just a hot bath but also an evening by the fire reading a good book.

Lighting also gave me new confidence in going out at night. After dinner with friends at a neighbouring bay, I drove back with assurance along the farm track towards the pinpoint of the outside light. Darkness in the country is complete, quite unlike that in the over-lit towns and now my one light pierced the enveloping black. As a lighthouse guided a sailor in the days before radar, so the light led me home and when I turned off the car headlights, instead of the usual thick blackness I had a well-lit path to the back door.

Besides lighting improvements, power gave me other options to make life on the farm easier and first among these was a pump. After some searching I found one capable of driving water from the rain tank to the feeder and Dee came over to help me install it, a job we managed with remarkable ease. Using Andy's generator every now and then to keep up the water supply had become quite a problem. I wasn't strong enough to pull the starter and relied on Andy or a visitor to get it going but the noise of its operation was so shattering to the quiet of the land I found myself reluctant to use it. My new pump, simple and almost silent, did the job in half the time. I got into a routine of filling the tank on the last day of a stay then if it used too much power there was time for it to build up again in my absence.

In those early days with solar power I was cautious in its use, not knowing its limits and frightened of draining the batteries. I was miserly with the lights, switching them off when they weren't essential and unplugging all appliances to ensure they were never left on. After one particularly vigilant night when Dee was staying she christened me the 'power police' and the name stuck. But with more experience came confidence. When I accidentally left the pump on for three hours instead of the normal 15 minutes, and even this didn't run me short of power, I realised my anxiety about the odd light bulb was entirely unnecessary and from then became, if not power greedy, then at least moderately voracious in its use.

Now, after living here for some years, I am super-confident with the solar power and have extended the system to two panels, using a small generator to top up the batteries in winter. I have a computer and stereo, a video and washing machine and even make the occasional use of an iron. Visitors hardly know they're in an alternative energy house though I still caution them to turn off lights when they're not in use and never leave anything on standby. I do get teased about the contradiction inherent in Cloud Farm being on solar power, but then I smile serenely and remind people that I never have a power bill. And there are days, when a snow-storm or wind gust cuts off power to the area, that my neighbours look longingly up the valley at the blazing lights. Maybe then they think I'm not quite as crazy as they feared.

However the system hasn't been completely trouble-free. Once I flattened the batteries by keeping a fridge running too long into the sun-shortened days of autumn — an exceptional Indian summer period lulled me into thinking I could risk it — but it's not the kind of mistake you make twice. Now I keep a close eye on the battery levels and pump them up with the generator if they need a boost, and I've bought a gas-powered fridge.

I've become good friends with the local supplier of solar equipment. My system is modest by his standards, but so successful that I've sent a few customers his way. As the price of electricity increases more people are interested in alternatives and I never tire of explaining to visitors how it all works and how easy it is to live in a solar powered house. I've never forgotten the kindness of Stuart who explained it all to me, and I try to emulate his attitude, even if my knowledge level is only a fraction of his.

Those last crucial steps

My ex-partner John is one of those rare people who enjoy helping others — either in a practical way or by offering a listening ear. He's a great conversationalist and during our years together we talked about everything but now, since we'd split up, he lived in Dunedin and our paths rarely crossed. So it was quite a coincidence that I suddenly received a call from him, just when I needed a guiding hand.

The year was passing but I hadn't been able to screw up the courage to tell the medical school of my impending retirement. I'd made the decision and I had no doubts it was the right one, but fear held me back from handing in my notice. It was a daunting prospect: the job was secure and well-paid with lots of perks and once I gave it up I'd have few other chances of employment. My spending power would be restricted forever. I was finding it hard to take that final step!

I'd told close friends of my plans and they were encouraging, but concerned for me too. They weren't game to dissuade me from my path, nor to push me along it. Giving up a professional career that took years to achieve wasn't something they'd done; they didn't know any more than I did how it would go. I began to procrastinate badly.

No one at work would have suspected I was contemplating change — there was nothing unusual in my behaviour. We were planning for the future development of the department, applying for big grants, appointing new staff; it all involved long-term strategising and the longer my deception continued the harder it got to say anything.

The call from John came out of the blue. We hadn't seen each other for three or four years, not since the time of our separation, but at that moment he was just the person I needed to talk with about my plans. He understood me well and knew my strengths and weaknesses, hopes and worries. We'd been through one or two hard times together and he'd never shirked from making difficult decisions, or from moving on when it was time to go. I could rely on him to give me an honest opinion.

We met for a meal and spent several hours together as I explained my plans and confessed my fears. He questioned and probed and reflected, helping me see the decision in its lifelong context, not focussing on short-term anxieties, real as they might be. In the process he reassured me, rebuilding my confidence and boosting my strength to get over the last, crucial hurdle.

But that's not all that happened. Meeting John again after that long break, I glimpsed my new self reflected in his eyes. I saw what huge changes had taken place since we'd been together, how far I'd moved on and what strengths and skills I'd developed. For the first time I realised what a gift our parting had been. It's so easy to be overwhelmed by grief when a relationship ends that you don't notice what opportunities are presented. Now I saw what a different person I'd become in the years on my own, how being single had allowed me to explore the capacities I'd put aside for the sake of a relationship and how fulfilled I felt as a result.

Buoyed up by all of this, I went into work the next day, made an appointment to see my boss and before the week was out I'd resigned. It wasn't easy — I was terrified on the day of the appointment — and my boss's reaction wasn't what I'd expected. Instead of admiring my bravery, or being sorry to see me go, he seemed genuinely puzzled by my decision and almost cross at the inconvenience it caused. The staff in my department were more understanding, surprised but applauding my decision, and several of them shared a secret desire to make similar lifestyle changes. Once all the paper work was complete and the resignation accepted my immediate feelings were of light-headedness and relief. I still had the rest of the year to see out, but the die was cast, the worst over and it would all be downhill from here.

With a new decisiveness and a spring in my step I set about the last jobs necessary to make Cloud Farm a permanent home. The most prosaic was to install a toilet.

When I bought the place there was no toilet, not even a long-drop. A shed at the bottom of the garden housed a plastic bucket underneath an appropriately shaped seat, but this 'toilet' was not fit for resurrection. On visits to the farm I made do with a variety of arrangements, none of them satisfactory — like going out into the bush or holding on until I got down to Akaroa. I was very familiar with the public toilets and chose my café on the quality of their toilet rather than their coffee. As soon as I began to stay overnight at the farm I invested in a chemical camping toilet which was a big improvement, particularly after dark, since sorties into the undergrowth were often cold and slippery.

But that too had its problems. Carrying the full tank up to the car was almost beyond me, and emptying its contents proved quite a challenge. They had to go down a sewerage system so the tank went back with me to the city where I had to find a ground-floor toilet. A friend offered hers but the job of disposal left an unpleasant tang in the air that I was reluctant to impose on her house.

Finally I found a satisfactory, if clandestine, solution. After my workmates had gone home for the night, I emptied the tank into the toilet at my department. The smell had dispersed by the time anyone started work again. But this procedure was not without adventure. Located in the central city, the department was next to residential houses and as I unloaded my cargo I worried about what the neighbours thought of this after-dark delivery service. It was hard to be subtle when I had to park as close as possible to the front door, unset the burglar alarm, switch on the lights, prop open all the doors between car and toilet, then dash in with the heavy load. The disposal itself, which I did taking hardly a breath, involved several flushings of the toilet and washings out of the tank.

This chemical contraption was a satisfactory, if burdensome, short-term solution but for full-time living on the farm I needed a real toilet. Most rural properties rely on septic tanks set into the ground while others have large holding tanks that must be emptied occasionally by big pumping trucks. Neither of these methods appealed, nor were they feasible: Cloud Farm lies on volcanic rock unsuitable for digging in a tank, and the pumping service requires access for large vehicles. Furthermore, both need a lot of water for flushing which would waste my precious supply.

The solution seemed to be a composting toilet, something I'd heard of but knew little about. I first tried one in Wales during my visit to Europe and found it was odourless and waterless. It seemed to perform just like an ordinary toilet except you threw in a handful of sawdust after use instead of pulling a chain.

I'd assumed composting toilets were rare in New Zealand, but on asking around found they were becoming more common, particularly for use in isolated locations. At the Hinewai Reserve, Hugh had one to serve an accommodation block which he invited me to inspect and take for a trial run. It was set in a small shed with a pitched roof. Inside the door you had to climb up three steps to reach the seat, which gave something of a royal ambience to the experience. Apparently this model needed a three-metre drop between pan and collection area so was probably ideal for a two-storied house. It seemed to work alright but I didn't want something you had to clamber up to. I had images of myself missing a step in the middle of the night and hitting my head on the toilet or the floor.

A friend in the Marlborough Sounds was involved in a trial of composting toilets around the walkway there and showed me the model being tested at the campsite near her house. It didn't have the access problem of Hugh's but there were one or two concerns: in the heavy-use period it got smelly and other times it got too dry to compost properly. This wasn't going to be the toilet for me either!

In Melbourne some months earlier I'd picked up a brochure on an Australian toilet and from somewhere amongst my papers it emerged. Contacting the Christchurch agent, I received a deluge of information: simple drawings, technical details, scientific papers, illustrations of applications and a video featuring satisfied customers. None of that was glossy or high tech; there was plenty of straightforward, practical information which, after I'd read through it, made a lot of sense. I called the agent to talk further and he invited me to meet the toilet's inventor who was visiting New Zealand the following month.

When the day came I had meetings all morning and teaching all afternoon, but I managed to escape for an early lunch break and drove to the suburb where the agent worked from his home. Here I found myself closeted in the garage with two large men who for the next hour discussed faeces, urine and compost as I nibbled my sandwich and apple. It was a somewhat surreal experience. But I was impressed with their professionalism and knowledge and left convinced this toilet would work. It was more expensive than others but in this area I was prepared to pay extra for performance!

Before going further I had to get a permit from the council to put in a composting toilet. They weren't common on Banks Peninsula and it was rumoured that approval was hard to obtain so I made a date with the local building inspector to ask his advice. Although sceptical at first, he agreed there were few alternatives for my site and confirmed the brand I proposed as the best choice, the council having recently installed one as a public toilet. He wasn't enthusiastic but I got a sense of grudging approval which, a few weeks later, translated into the required permissions.

Andy, willing as ever to try something he hadn't done before, agreed to install the toilet and took all the technical drawings and brochures home to study. He offered to collect the toilet from the Lyttleton wharf where it had been shipped from Australia. His van was completely filled with the bits and pieces including a huge composting tank with segmented inside and a porcelain toilet pan much like any other but without the curved bottom. When I next got to the farm everything was sitting on the verandah in large cartons and containers.

The toilet was to be housed in the back shed and required a hole under the floor of about one cubic metre — a digging job that would have taken me months of weekend work. Luckily I had a friend, Noel, who owed me a favour and he volunteered to come over and do it. For several hours he laboured while I kept my fingers crossed; there were some huge boulders around and if he ran into one that was immovable we'd be in serious trouble. But luck was with him; he dug both the hole and an access way without major problems. All was now ready for the installation.

It may seem crazy to have put a toilet in the back shed when winter temperatures were close to freezing and rain common. I hadn't wanted this and had spent many months fruitlessly devising ways to keep it inside the house. But a composting toilet without mains power needs the warmth of a north-facing wall and there was none available, all being in the living area or kitchen. So reluctantly I decided to use the back shed — which meant cold and wet extremities on some nights. Many years later I came up with a solution: the passage between house and back shed was converted to a sun porch that allowed under-cover access which, although chilly in winter, is always dry and draught-free.

Andy and Noel spent a whole day installing the toilet, packing it with insulation and putting an outlet through the roof to discourage smells. A strange glass-fronted box holding a coil of large-gauge piping was the passive-heating system attached to the north wall and designed to take warm air across the toilet tank and help with the evaporation of liquids. The access way to the tank was closed off with a pair of small doors and after painting these and the hot box the same colour as the shed, we had a neat professional finish both inside and out.

With beer in hand we admired the finished job but no one volunteered for the ceremonial first use. When the men had gone I performed that ritual alone.

It was great to have a toilet under cover, one you didn't have to empty at the end of a stay, that could be used exactly as an ordinary toilet except there was no flushing. All you had to do was put a handful of popcorn down once a week and as the pan had come packaged in acres of the stuff, there was enough to last me several years. I put this into large plastic bags and stored it in the roof space where I hoped it would never be discovered by passing rats — that could turn the house into a rodent version of McDonald's.

With its new toilet, the shed had to be made more user-friendly; it needed a proper floor and some lining on the walls. Dee found me trailer loads of polystyrene offcuts for insulation and I spent several weekends closeted with the toilet in the back shed, cutting sheets of it to size and wedging them into the spaces between joists in walls and ceiling. This was the longest period of time I was likely to spend there; if the toilet was going to smell this was when I'd notice it, but never did I get a whiff of anything. It seemed to be performing perfectly.

Andy came over for a day and together we did the walls and floor, hauling out his generator to run the skilsaw for cutting boards to the size and shape required. As usual I was impressed by the speed and concentration with which he worked. He stopped only for a lunch break and otherwise moved quickly from one task to the next, determined to finish the job by the end of the day.

Andy's business was growing as his reputation spread. When we first started on this house together he was in the early stages of setting up, but now his days were increasingly booked. Seeing the speed and energy with which he attacked jobs, I understood why his quotes were so competitive. It made me realise again how lucky I'd been to meet him when I did, with the house in need of the sort of devotion that Andy could give and his business small enough to allow him the time for it. But both had developed together and, like an adolescent, the house was needing Andy less and less, though it was not yet ready for full independence.

Making the break

I celebrated my 50th birthday in a log cabin in the outback of British Columbia. With two of my closest friends, Nedra and Rosemary, I flew to Vancouver then drove north for three days to the tiny settlement of Nimpo Lake. From there we travelled about an hour in a float-plane to land on a small lake 5000 feet above sea-level, surrounded by mountains. This was the home of author, Chris Czajkowski.

During a visit to my Uncle John in Vancouver he'd introduced me to the writings of Chris, an English woman who'd gone to live on her own in the depths of Northern Canada. She built a couple of log cabins and survived by living simply, earning an income from writing about life in the wilderness and taking in a few visitors during the summer.

Her story had inspired and stayed with me so that when it came to deciding how to celebrate my 50th I knew exactly what I wanted to do. A few years earlier I'd have invited a large group of friends to an inner city restaurant. Now I wanted to be altogether wilder, closer to nature and further from civilisation. Through my uncle I made contact with Chris and arranged to spend a week there over the period of my birthday. Persuading Nedra and Rosemary to come too was surprisingly easy. They'd both had their 50ths some years before and were up for any adventure, particularly if it involved travelling and celebrating.

We arrived at Vancouver airport in a state of great excitement, carrying a crate of Lindauer and a home-baked birthday cake, both of which caused the Customs and Agriculture Authorities minor heart attacks. Apparently you can take only one bottle of wine duty-free into Canada and food that is not pre-packaged is treated with the suspicion conferred on a potential parcel bomb. But somehow, after much talking, we managed to get both through. Our story of three middle-aged women on such a mission melted the resolve of even the most seasoned officials. My poor uncle, waiting in the Arrivals hall while every other passenger emerged from the Customs tunnel, had decided we were being strip-searched and possibly in serious trouble.

The unnamed lake where Chris lives is 40 miles south of Lonesome Lake in the foothills of the Pacific Coast Range. Three days' walk from the nearest road, its isolation was well beyond the experience or comfort zone of us New Zealanders. We shared our cabin with pack rats — about the size of possums only much faster — and the lake with grizzly bears, which we never met face to face, but we were ever conscious of their presence, particularly as Chris had regaled us with horrifying stories of cabin break-ins and unexpected attacks. Mosquitoes and tiny biting insects, aptly called 'no-see-ums', were our constant companions, driving us often to wear the ridiculous body-encasing nets which we'd been persuaded to bring. The only tracks through the thick surrounding forest were those created by moose or caribou so we rarely left the safety of the lakeside unless accompanied by Chris and her dogs.

I gained a new appreciation for our benign New Zealand bush where the weather is our only danger and even that will only keep us hutbound for a week or so. Here, in winter, Chris could spend four or five months snowed into her cabin. We learnt to paddle the large open canoes that were her only form of transport and to bath in a small washing tub with water brought up in buckets from the lake's edge. The toilet was primitive by anybody's standards and we used it always under the watchful eyes of the squirrels in the trees above.

When the birthday came it was celebrated in style. Chris baked fresh bread and Rosemary cooked a cordon bleu feast, creating magic from the few stores we'd laboriously carried in. We consumed Lindauer in copious quantities and Nedra's hard-won birthday cake provided the climax of the night.

I was beginning a new chapter in my life. What Chris was doing was infinitely braver than anything I might attempt. Strong, talented and independent, she was happiest when reliant only on herself for company. I could never emulate her life — nor did I want to — but it was an inspiration, giving me confidence that if she, a woman of my age and similar background, could be this brave, then surely I could tackle the easier and more comfortable task I had set myself.

Returning to Vancouver via float-plane, ferries and islands, we drank the final bottle of bubbly with my uncle as we demolished the last of the birthday cake and told him endless tales of our adventures. He seemed almost relieved to deliver us unharmed back to the airport and our flight home.

As soon as I could I went out to Cloud Farm where it was cold, the land still patched with melting snow, the insipid sky threatening drizzle. But I was not put off; I needed to spend a night there to reassure myself about the innocuous isolation and relative safety of my future home.

I was easily convinced. Despite the engine-challenging climb, the farm was only 15 minutes from the nearest shops — the sort of separation from humanity that I could manage. And the only wildlife interested in my presence were the fantails diving after insects I disturbed. The house was cold at first, but the log-burner was soon roaring and the kettle whistling, while in the shed a green glow showed the batteries were fully charged and the toilet in the corner was under cover and odourless. Who could want more? I spent a cosy night reading late in front of the fire and I slept long and soundly.

Next morning I inspected the new track through the bush. During my time away one of Hugh's helpers on the reserve had extended and reformed it so that you could walk right through to the paddock on the other side. With great excitement I started along the track, winding past the old toilet spot and squeezing through gaps between huge old trees, until it suddenly ended almost at the same spot as before. Here I found a note from Pete the worker pinned to a fuchsia, saying he'd discovered a much better route so instead of extending this one he'd put in a new track higher up.

Initially I was a bit peeved, not sure I wanted a whole new track somewhere else, but I followed his directions and was soon walking along a gently sloping path where mosses cascaded from branches above and lichens patterned old stumps and rocks lining the edges. It wound under trees and through ferns. The bush occasionally opened up to give glimpses of sea and headlands far below. The track finally emerged onto open grassland that looked straight down into the bay. I leaned against a dead trunk and contemplated my new vista. Who could be cross when such a wonderful track, so carefully crafted, was the result of a bit of initiative?

It was one of those defining moments when I suddenly realised how far I'd come. Not only was the house liveable but now I could begin to enjoy its surroundings as well. I got in touch with Pete and congratulated him on his work, but it wasn't until many years later, when I'd built tracks of my own through the bush, that I truly appreciated what a great job he'd done.

Cloud Farm was almost ready for permanent habitation but one final piece of technology, a phone, was required before it was complete. I'd taken my cellphone to try out reception and found it worked in the topmost corner of the property but not at the house. This was better than nothing; when staying a day or two it let me keep some contact with the outside world. I got into the habit of walking Vita in the evenings, stopping at this high point to watch the sunset and make any calls to friends or workmen. Occasionally a farmer would drive past me on a gate talking to my phone — probably more evidence of my strange ways.

But in the long term this cellphone arrangement was not viable. I needed a phone nearer than the hilltop paddock. I'd already discovered this when I woke one morning feeling soggy, then developed flu but couldn't face the trek to the high point to phone out. For several days I lay almost comatose, not really needing anyone or anything but still wishing someone knew I was so ill.

I also wanted a phone for my computer since I relied on email for communicating with students and workmates as well as friends. I wondered if it was a luxury I could do without, but I wanted solitude not isolation, separation from the world, not to be cut off from it. A phone was essential.

I called up Telecom for a quote and discovered again the exorbitant cost of utilities in our post-1980s free market economy. Only a year or two earlier, when Telecom was still a state-owned company, the connection would have been free; now they must charge. Their technician came to the farm but the news was all bad: no phone lines in the area meant they'd have to install a radio-operated phone (imported from Australia) to bounce the signal off a nearby receiver. I'd need solar panels and batteries for powering it all. The total cost would be almost $20,000 and of this they would expect me to pay about $6000.

I sought several people's advice. Communications technology was developing fast; it would be cheaper to put in a cellphone repeater giving reception to the house, and in only a year or two internet access via cellphone would be possible. But this didn't appeal; I was against the additional cost for those calling me and I needed to make use of the cheap international service. Another adviser said I was lucky Telecom were offering to pay any of the cost and soon they'd be quoting the full $20,000 for such a job. I decided, reluctantly, to accept their quote.

It took them several months to get the equipment and the necessary resource consents through but finally the day came when they met me at the farm to install the system. The three-day job involved four men and several pieces of heavy machinery which made some sense of the high cost. First came a large truck to drill a post hole. After some false starts they managed to find a gap between the rocks to get down to the required depth. The pole, lowered and cemented in, stood six or seven metres above ground and half as much again below. They attached an aerial to this and on a nearby ridge erected a special transmitter angled towards it. The solar panels were also hung on the pole which was crowned with a tall earthing rod — they weren't going to let lightning destroy all their equipment! Next morning there was more digging, to bury all the wires connecting the panels to the battery-powered radio set which was housed in the back shed. When the technician arrived he wired it all up, installing the radio set and connecting all the various bits. By about four p.m. on the third day I had a phone.

That night I made one or two calls to friends but it was hard to realise the situation had changed. Then I rang my sister, looking out at the view as I spoke to her in Spain and, connecting up the laptop, I emailed my brother in England and my uncle in Canada. There was still solitude and peace at the farm but there was no longer a feeling of isolation. It appealed to me that in this house which until recently had seen neither power nor running water, I could sit in comfort and surf the net or advise my students on their research problems. The farm still felt remote and not quite part of the 20th century, yet as we approached the 21st, I could sit in the kitchen or even in the back shed, and communicate with the world.

At first I regretted the intrusion when the phone rang and pierced the silence: it could so quickly transport me from the peace of the farm to the hassle and rush of the world outside, draw me into other's worries and anxieties when I'd come here to escape them. But I learned to accept this as a small price to pay for the contact it gave me. It was easy to switch off once the call was over and let calm return. Irrespective of the news from over the hill or across the sea, the birds sang on and the sun kept shining or the rain falling — this somehow kept things in perspective. Nature's imperviousness to the problems of the world provided sharp contrast to the way stresses were exacerbated in the city. There crises fed on themselves and multiplied, stirred up by the media or the rumourmongers. Here they were absorbed by the green and the silence, so that they shrank and retreated and were soon grown over.

Speaking to people on the phone I began to notice their impatience with me if they called with a particularly pressing problem and I failed to be wound up by it or didn't seem to appreciate what they could see as its dire consequences. I was still a part of that world but I was less and less in the role it expected of me.

By now it was three years since I'd bought the farm and what had been little more than a cowshed was a warm, dry house wired up for contemporary living. The renovation work wasn't complete, there was still an endless string of jobs to do, but the house was transformed. Now it was time to transform my life.

I paid the major bills and did my calculations again. I'd have to practise simple living from now on; there'd be few luxuries and no extravagances, but I was happy to sacrifice such things to regain my life. Time would be my own. I could daydream all day if I wished. The purpose behind all this: to reclaim my head as well as my life.

I was to leave work on the first of February. I spent the whole of January clearing out my office. After seventeen years my papers and books had accumulated to an unmanageable level but with the help of others I threw out and sorted until finally there was only a small collection of box files and reference books to store in my garage. What had been a warm, sunny, welcoming office became a cold, clinical space; the first stage in my separation from work was complete.

The department held a party and gave me a beautiful stone gecko that was to bask in the sun amongst the rocks at the farm and remind me I'd chosen life in the slow lane. Then there were the formal farewells. I'd spent more than half my working life at the school and it was hard to leave but these functions helped in the process of severing connections and closing that chapter of my life.

Feeling calm and content with my decision, I moved out to the farm in the first week of retirement, finding someone to rent my apartment in the city but keeping the garage for storage and the hayloft room above as a bolthole. If the farm got too cold in winter or I felt too isolated then this would be my escape. But now, in February, it was warm and sunny, the sun rose soon after six and set around nine and the days were not long enough for all I had to do.

Heather arrives

Exactly a year later in the summer of 1999 I met Heather and, looking back, it's obvious that Cloud Farm was ready for her since the next stage of its restoration would require another sort of person. But at the time I wasn't aware that either I, or Cloud Farm, needed her. On the contrary, we seemed to be getting along fine on our own and progressing steadily, if slowly.

That first year after leaving work I managed a happy balance between mental and physical activity. I grew a few plants for my yet-undesigned garden, dug seedlings from the bush and potted them up ready for transplanting. I learnt how to propagate natives from their seeds, turning the back shed into a mini nursery with trays on every surface. Out the front of the house I planted a bed of various tussocks and tried to lay down some rudimentary paths. Instead of lawn I put in dozens of the small Banks Peninsula blue tussock hoping they would remain compact — I had no intention of mowing lawns or tidying edges like someone in the suburbs.

On colder days I began researching the history of the farm, starting with old land deeds and electoral rolls in the public library, then closeting myself in the back room of the local museum to read through early issues of the *Akaroa Mail*, searching for any references to the families who'd lived here. And I started writing this book, spending a mandatory couple of hours on it every day.

I had not a moment's regret; the life I'd created seemed everything I wanted. Weather, not the demands of my diary, dictated the rhythm of the day. Buying a cappuccino became a treat, not a necessity to get me through the next hour of work. I gradually lost touch with my work colleagues and quickly forgot the names of all those committees on which I'd spent so much of my time. Coping on my greatly reduced income was not difficult, my everyday expenses being small and the need for luxuries rare. I had clothes and shoes to last for years and even enough frequent flyer points for a spell in a warmer climate during the worst of winter.

But it wasn't all plain sailing. There were times of loneliness, worry and frustration. When the first big storm hit the farm I felt very scared and alone. The house gave no cause for concern — it remained solid as ever — but I wasn't sure about the huge trees beside it, as branches flew off, ripped away like broccoli pieces to crash on the ground below. When the wind grew stronger and the light faded I worried that whole trees might blow over and crush the house. But I sat out the night, drifting off to sleep from time to time in front of the log-burner with Vita curled up for comfort at my side. By dawn it was still again and I reminded myself that these trees had withstood the wind for a hundred years already.

Sometimes I felt frustrated by my weaknesses — when my physical skills didn't match the demands of the rigorous country life. The legacy of my childhood polio had rarely inconvenienced me in the city, but here on Cloud Farm some tasks were beyond me. I could spend a whole day stacking a load of firewood and I got very tired carrying things from one part of the farm to another. I was hardy and determined, but I had to admit I was a bit weak.

Of course there were ways round this problem: waiting until someone visited before tackling things I couldn't manage on my own; or Andy would come for a day and undertake a hundred jobs in no time at all, but this made me feel uncomfortably dependent and not the totally capable person I'd assumed I would be.

There were also times of loneliness and these took me by surprise. You'd think I might have anticipated this, suddenly switching from a busy demanding life to one of isolation in the bush, but I'd never considered it. In the city I'd had so many friends and commitments that I often longed for a day alone, never considering there could be a downside to that. But now I knew no one, had no demands placed on me and had to actively seek out company when my own began to pall. Luckily I met one or two long-time residents of Akaroa who introduced me to others so that I gradually began to recognise faces on the street and to have homes where I was welcome to drop in. But I kept in touch with many of my Christchurch friends. Either they visited Cloud Farm or I went to them for a couple of days of concentrated socialising before I returned to my solitary life.

The next twist in Cloud Farm's fate occurred during one of these visits to Christchurch. I was at an impromptu dinner party where the conversation was a bit flat, the food rather flaccid and the room slightly too small for the number of guests. It was nobody's fault. We'd spread out a picnic to enjoy 'Opera in the Park', when sudden last-minute rain cancelled the event.

Nothing daunted, we packed our sodden quiches and flattened bubbly off to somebody's nearby apartment but it was an anticlimax to say the least. We'd anticipated the voice of Malvina Major; now with only ourselves to listen to, our spirits were as damp as the picnic rugs, our minds as dull as the half-eaten food.

Perhaps hoping for distraction, someone asked me to recount how I found Cloud Farm and moved there to live — it was still recent enough to be a source of interest. I was probably about half way through the story when a hand jerked over the table, its finger pointing at me almost accusingly as a voice demanded, 'When can I come to Cloud Farm?' The look in the blue eyes shining across at me implied that their owner should have been included in this adventure. A hush fell over the room, a shock of silence, as I stopped mid-sentence. This was almost inappropriate behaviour, though we didn't actually have rules and we had drunk quite a bit of wine. But for a stranger to interrupt like this was a bit unusual. Most of us knew each other well and attended this event together every year, but my friend Sue had brought her neighbour, a smiling, blonde woman whom few of us had met before. So far she'd seemed happy to sit quietly on the edges of conversations; now she had issued a challenge. With no time to think, I instinctively grabbed the proffered hand and called her bluff. 'Tomorrow?' I asked.

The moment passed and the evening continued as if nothing had happened, but I was a bit rattled, unused to having strangers accost me or foist themselves on me as guests.

Not quite next day, but the next weekend, Sue brought her neighbour, Heather Chapman, out to the farm for the promised visit. In the meantime, I'd found out a bit about her. Heather was my age, the deputy principal of a country school north of the city, and a talented artist. Energetic and athletic, she packed her life with jogging and yoga as well as keeping her classroom of children happy and the school running successfully. And, contrary to the impression she made at the dinner party, she was quite shy and retiring, preferring solitude to socialising.

Heather emerged from Sue's car looking as expectant as a ten-year-old about to go for her first horse ride. She'd spent her early years on a farm so this escape to rural isolation promised a return to the blissful days of childhood.

The evening was still and almost balmy as I took them through the bush track and out into the sudden clearing with its long vista to the sea below. Perched like seagulls along an old tree trunk, we watched the sky change from smoky blue to deep red. I often came to this spot for a drink before dinner; there were glasses and bottles hidden in the hollow of a nearby stump. I poured everyone their favourite, and we sat sipping our cocktails as if on the poop deck of a luxury liner. After only a short time the view and stillness lulled us into the sort of calm that follows a long and luxurious massage. When at last we reluctantly left the scene, it was almost too dark to find our way back through the bush.

Heather was from Southland where you never go anywhere without plenty of food so she and Sue had come laden with breads, cheeses and pies, enough to feed several families. That night we ate heartily and long into the night and there were enough leftovers that even Vita was impressed with this new visitor.

Sleeping late the next morning, I emerged dozy and bleary to make breakfast for my guests, but I was much too slow off the mark. They'd cooked toast, found my muesli, and Heather had already scrambled up to the ridge top to do her yoga exercises as the sun rose from the sea. I wondered briefly if life on the farm was making me lazy or whether this woman was just an exercise fanatic, but as she thrust a hot coffee into my hands I quickly gave up thinking about it.

That day the three of us worked around the farm together, carting rocks up from the lower slopes to make my tussock garden look more interesting. Heather took over its design and transformed the bland, shapeless space into one of contrasts and contours. After lunch she got on the roof, jumping up like a gazelle, to clear the gutters — a job I couldn't do easily and didn't like doing alone. Later as we walked on the ridge tops taking photos of regenerating bush, her artistic eye picked out angles and perspectives that I would never have noticed.

They left in the early evening and the farm fell silent in a way I hadn't experienced before. Over a pre-dinner drink on the verandah, I surveyed my now beautiful tussock garden and contemplated the day. It hit me suddenly how much potential there still was to be discovered and developed at Cloud Farm, how a different eye could see so much more for the place than I could envisage with my limited perspective. I was confident about design inside the house, but I realised how hopeless I'd been on the outside, dawdling about in the garden without any real vision. Now, in one short day, this stranger had created beauty in some areas and shown me the potential of others. And I realised another thing — I'd enjoyed Heather's company, her enthusiasm, energy and light-heartedness and she'd seemed to love the farm as much as I did. Driving off, she asked if she could come again and I readily agreed. The thought of her spending more time here lifted a weight from my heart I hadn't even known was there.

From then on Heather came to the farm most weekends, at first helping with essential jobs, then taking over whole projects. She established a vegetable garden on the top level above the house, building on some broken-down beds unearthed from beneath great clumps of grass. Then she laid paths all over the place, linking one area of the garden to another, making it easier and safer to get around. Plants I'd carefully nurtured from seedlings now came into their own as whole new garden areas were created for mass plantings of my nursery protégées.

Most of the time we worked together, Heather having the ideas and I helping carry them out, but Cloud Farm played its part too. A job was no sooner begun than the farm rewarded us with a revelation of its hidden beauties. Like the day we started clearing from close to the house a mass of creepers, mostly bush lawyer and muehlenbeckia. It was one of those jobs that seemed so overwhelming I'd never got started on it. The going was tough. With goggles and thick gloves to protect us from the sharp, springy tendrils, we removed piles and piles without noticeable effect. But in time we could see through the thick tangle to the trunks of big, old fuchsias, gnarled and twisted around monstrous boulders that were encrusted with mosses and lichens. This looked like part of a primeval forest; these rocks were the spewings of the volcano from which the peninsula was formed thousands of years before. We cut away all the lower branches of the fuchsias revealing the line of their trunks. Here was a beautiful feature garden of the kind that the most ambitious landscape architect in Fendalton or Remuera could only dream about. In one weekend the job was complete. As well as revealing this magnificent area, we'd saved several young totara from smothering and given the house and garden better definition, separating them out from the bush.

Another day we unearthed huge old barrel-shaped blocks of concrete. They'd been formed many years earlier when dry cement in barrels became wet and set hard. The wooden struts had rotted away, leaving only their imprint on the outside. These 'barrels' were so heavy they were almost immovable — even with Heather's strength and determination — but with help we managed to salvage them to use as magnificent plinths for outdoor sculptures or good solid bases for picnic tables.

I don't want to give the impression that our time together was all work. We often stopped early at the end of the day and filled up the old bath on the verandah — I'd connected up an outside hot-water tap for just this purpose. With a welcome aperitif in hand we could soak tired muscles and watch the sky change hues or the moon rise from the sea. Many days we simply explored the farm and its tracks, enjoying the bush and views, whilst speculating about where new tracks could go. We were happy in the simplicity of our weekend lives and the intrinsic satisfaction of hard work.

During the week Heather returned to her teaching and I eased back to a more leisurely pace, writing, reading and pottering around outside. We went on like this for almost a year, with Heather travelling back and forth from North Canterbury each weekend, but at the end of this she gave up her job and moved out to Cloud Farm. It was a big wrench for her to leave after 17 years at the same school but she felt just as confident as I had two years before, that Cloud Farm was where her future lay. She rented out her house, packed her belongings, brought over Marley, her Burmese cat, and began a new life on the peninsula.

The farmhouse was too small for all of us and our activities. We put up a painting studio for Heather on the flat area above the house. I designed a simple structure with a concrete floor and pitched roof, which Andy built. Clad in corrugated iron, it resembled a barn and was in keeping with the rest of the farm; with old windows and French doors on the seaward side and a large bi-folding window on the sunny side, it had both light and views. Heated with a small log-burner and powered by a simple solar system, the studio, when it was finally complete, was about as cosy as the house and the views from it even more dramatic.

We built a smaller studio for me on a level piece of ground just below the house. A much less ambitious project, it was a converted garden shed with lots of windows, but it was just as appealing with equally magnificent views. An old kerosene heater I'd bought in an antique shop many years before did a great job of warming it even in the coldest days of winter.

The next stage of life at Cloud Farm began; my solitary quiet was supplanted by hammering and laughter, and the landscape around the house changed dramatically as Heather let her creative talents and energy go wild.

She constructed a large koru-shaped garden near her studio, using various stones, gravels and rocks in its design. It led naturally into a boulder garden with astelias, tussocks and rengarenga rock lilies, the bright red of lichen on the boulders reflected in plantings of red flaxes and cabbage trees, giving an effect of subtlety and contrasting textures. We discovered that the rare Akaroa daisy loved our climate and soon had whole banks covered with its marvellous foliage, growing the plants from seeds which Hugh gave us.

For better access we put in a gentle, winding track joining these gardens and the studio to the main house, a job we could never have done without the help of our eighty-year-old friend, Johnny, after whom we named it.

My half-hearted attempts to establish a green of low-growing tussocks in front of the house were abandoned and the area put down in lawn. Heather was happy to mow it, deriving great satisfaction from the contrast between the controlled neat lines of the lawn and the untamed russet and brown grasses in the tussock garden. Behind the house the rough pasture, when attacked with a weed-eater, revealed an overgrown orchard that we subsequently tried to nurture into fruit-bearing but without great success.

For many months Heather put aside her painting to concentrate on the gardens, devising areas to complement the house and its bush surround as well as to link them together in an apparently seamless way. She was energetic and unstoppable, impatient to see progress and constantly frustrated by the slow growth rate of plants at this height. But, little by little, Cloud Farm began to change until the whole property, not just the house, looked loved and cared-for as it had probably not since its first owners left eighty years earlier.

With Heather taking up residence, I noticed my acceptance into the area began to change subtly for the better. She taught part-time at some of the local schools and became well known to children and their parents, the role of the primary school teacher being an important one in a small community. Perhaps too, people began to hear about the work we were doing at Cloud Farm which earned us their respect and interest, for within a short time we seemed to have become fully-fledged members of the peninsula community, invited to join all the local events and activities.

The garden tour

A year or so later there was another major twist in the destiny of Cloud Farm and its inhabitants and even though, looking back, it is easy to see the pattern developing, at the time we were taken by surprise.

I was at home alone one October night when the call came. 'It's not so much a garden tour, more an off-road experience. We don't expect show gardens, people will be coming just to see the view and the setting and to find out about your solar power and stuff.' That's how Suzanne persuaded me to let Cloud Farm become a venue for an 'Off-the-Beaten-Track Garden Tour' she was organising as a fund-raiser for the local school. I tried to stall her, saying I needed to discuss it with Heather, but you don't mess with Suzanne. She's the local doctor and a linchpin of the community who doesn't take 'no' for an answer.

So on the 1st of December 2001, seven years to the day since I bought a derelict house in the midst of a run-down farm, 220 people from all over the South Island paid good money to come and view it.

It's a nerve-wracking affair, being open to the public. You may know yourself how dreadful something has looked in the past and, by comparison, how good it looks now; you may be able to imagine how wonderful a newly planted area will look in a year's time, but outsiders judge things as they find them in the snapshot view they have on that particular day. We tried to see the garden as it would look to strangers and grew more anxious. I could tell the pressure was building on Heather by the frequency of lawn mowing and the frenetic pace of weeding as the open day approached. The garden wasn't my creation, it was hers — she felt it was her artistic talent on the line, not mine. By then she'd been in residence two years, not much time to convert barren scrubby hillsides into gardens and paths, particularly when she used only native plants which are notoriously slow to establish, and was working with volcanic soil in subalpine temperatures.

We planned well for the invasion of visitors; we marked out a route they were to follow, drew them a map for guidance and had walking sticks for them to borrow as required. After parking in the top paddock, they were to come down Beech Track which meanders through regenerating bush to the flat area in front of the studio. There Heather would meet them, explain a little about the place, then direct them down Johnny's Track to the house. Stationed there, I would show them around the house and surrounding gardens before sending them back up to Heather via Totara Track, a steepish path through the original bush, so that she could show them the top gardens then point them back up to their cars.

Our strategy was organised with military precision and for the first hour or so proceeded accordingly. The weather was ideal — sunny but with a nice breeze keeping the temperature down. People dribbled in a couple at a time and seemed suitably impressed; they asked interested questions and wanted to see everything they could before they went on their way. It was still early in the day; they had ten other gardens to see and lots of miles to drive between them. So far so good. Heather and I began to relax and even to enjoy ourselves.

About midday the pace hotted up and the atmosphere began to change. It started when two fashionably dressed women from Christchurch stepped delicately off the track looking as though the Merivale shopping mall was the biggest walk they usually tackled. But appearances can be deceptive. They raved about the house and its views, and when they reached the front verandah they sank into the large chairs, declaring, 'This is paradise'. They vowed they wouldn't leave. The flow of visitors built up and before I knew it there were about 20 people in the house, all asking questions, and a further 20 on the verandah or in the garden. None showed any signs of moving on. Little parties of four or five sat in the various view spots. All the garden chairs were taken and the song of the bellbirds was almost drowned by the murmurs of contentment and exclamations of joy issuing from the crowds.

This set the pattern for the rest of the day. The two women finally vacated their verandah seats, but were quickly replaced by others and the small groupings of people changed in composition as new arrivals pressured the overstayers to carry on, but everyone seemed to feel the same way. They were impressed by what we'd done, they gave us lots of praise and encouragement, but mainly they were overwhelmed by the sense of calm and peace that Cloud Farm and its views afforded, and happy just to sit about relaxing, perhaps contemplating for a little while what life could be like.

By the end of the day, when the organisers finally shut the

gate and took away the sign, Heather and I were both euphoric and exhausted but another hour was to pass before the last person left and we could flop into our well-warmed verandah chairs with our longed-for beers and begin to wind down.

We spent the next day like zombies, not even bothering to dress but just sitting about enjoying the silence. I felt as if I'd been at a ten-hour cocktail party with no nibbles or alcohol, but with that same intensity of social interaction. We were drained and depleted, hungover from the adrenalin excess of the occasion.

But the Garden Tour was a real turning point in our lives and Cloud Farm's, affirming our belief there is something very special here. We saw how pleasurable, even therapeutic, the visit was for some people and we understood for the first time that the farm with its magnificent bush and views might offer something beneficial for others as well as for ourselves. I'd always felt I wanted to help the land recover its original vegetation but I'd never thought before of sharing it with others.

Although we'd always had a sense of purpose, that sense was now emboldened — even if we didn't know yet how it would be realised. In the following months we worked with increased zeal, and the weather rewarded us with an ideal growing summer — wet and warm. We watched the precious plantings that had sat dormant for years begin to shoot up and out, taking on a healthy glow of satisfaction with their environment.

With the gardens going so well, Heather could devote more of her energies to the bush and hill surrounds, making several new tracks that linked up to form a network of walks. One goes up and over the ridge tops, following gentle contours and exposing the walker to magnificent views, and breezes, on all sides. It returns to the house through rain forest where the trees are festooned so thickly with mosses and epiphytes that their own forms are completely disguised. We took to walking this every night, its slope so gentle that even I could not complain about going up and down hill all the time. And of course, en route was the drinks cache so there was always that to look forward to!

Then she put in a big circular walk that meanders down to the forestry plantations through paddocks of regenerating bush. It returns via a newly bulldozed track through the tallest and oldest gorse where signs of natives coming through the undergrowth are already apparent. This is the walk the dogs most enjoyed, with its possum smells and long open vistas that offered a good stretch of the legs and the possibility that a rabbit would appear at any moment. (By now we had two dogs, Vita having been joined by Millie, another Tibetan terrier, named for the Millennium and a present for Heather on her 50th birthday.)

With tracks well established we turned our attention to the small semicircular grass hillside which rose to the bush line behind Heather's studio. I'd always loved this little patch. It was enclosed and protected by the surrounding trees yet it looked out over the full panorama of the Pacific Ocean far below. The idea came to us as we were putting a wide deck around the studio — useful for outside meals, we thought; but one day we reconfigured it as a concert platform, with one area for the string quartet or the baby grand and another for the singer, with the hillside above for the audience. We called up Kevin, the landscaping digger driver, who soon converted the rough hillside into tiered terraces with what would be garden beds at the lowest level. Heather constructed steps up the middle, reusing some old totara fence posts for the job, and we lined them with little white parahebes. Once the grasses have covered the terraces, the hebe hedges have thickened and the Akaroa daisies in the beds are in flower, we will hold an Opera in the Clouds.

The farm and its elements gave us the next direction for its development. We were celebrating the opening of a new track, a walkway between us and the Hinewai Reserve. We'd invited everyone likely to use the track to its opening then strung a ribbon across at its highest point and taken up several bottles of champagne. But the toasts had just begun when the clouds came down — so thick we could hardly see each other across the picnic rugs — but no one moved or complained and the ceremony ran its course, ending with a symbolic first walk to the house. The fog kept each of us close on the heels of the person ahead so we wouldn't lose the way. From Heather's thank you speech the idea emerged: inspired by the misty atmosphere and the spirit of the gathering she challenged us all to hold a banquet on the ridge top the following summer, irrespective of the weather.

When the time came, everyone rose to the occasion. Our neighbour Frank made a huge table from one of his trees and other neighbours used pulleys, ropes and a skilfully driven truck to help us get it into position. The diners each brought a chair that they'd made out of old stumps or driftwood so that the banquet setting looked like something straight out of *The Lord of the Rings.* The wind that night was so strong we couldn't stand upright, but we loved it — the gale only added to the romance and drama of the occasion. We had a genuine Scottish piper to remind Heather of her heritage as well as jugglers and musical contributions between courses.

Now the spot is available for celebrations of all sorts. At Easter last year we lined the track with candles and the local church held a dawn service here. In perfect weather, 30 people watched the sun rise slowly out of the sea to reflect its rays back to us from the snowy slopes of Aoraki/Mt Cook in the far distance. The ground sparkled with early frost and the stillness allowed the candles to flicker gently, their brightness fading as the sun's grew. It was one of those magical experiences you know you'll never forget and we ended it with barbecued fish, fresh French bread and steaming coffee.

Word spread about Cloud Farm and people began to call up and ask if they could walk over our tracks, the solitude and the magnificent views tempting them to chance it with winds and mists. Eventually we decided to offer guided walks for tourists so they could get right up onto the ridge tops and explore the views and the bush in safety while learning something of the history and ecology of the area. We've had people from all over the world and of most ages and their reactions always seem to be positive, their comments interesting. I liked the one from a retired airport manager in England: 'What on earth do you do for stress up here?'

And so Cloud Farm evolves. It seems that our role is to nurture and protect it for now and to share with others all that it has to offer.

We never run out of ideas — or rather, Cloud Farm never

stops putting them in our path. Like the day we came past the old quarry, an overgrown rocky formation on our western boundary. There amongst dead pine trunks and wild broom sat an elderly seagrass chair, looking as though its occupant had just gone off to make herself a cup of tea. (It had probably been dumped at the nearby rubbish skip and blown over the road.) We grabbed the chair which was just right for one of our outdoor areas, but seeing it there had given us a new perspective on the quarry — it too could be a wonderful sitting spot. Now our plans are to make it into a public park with picnic tables and a formed path so that people can reach its highest point and enjoy the stunning vistas on all sides. We want to name it the 'Elsie Keegan Lookout' after the first child born and raised at Cloud Farm at the turn of the century who gave so much to the Akaroa community in her long lifetime there. After her fiancée died in the First World War, she never married, but ever after described herself as 'undiscovered treasure' — a term we feel applies equally to Cloud Farm.

Epilogue

Some time after I gave up work and moved out to Cloud Farm I was back in the city for a brief visit when I ran into one of my more sophisticated and successful friends. She's the sort of woman whose face is fashionably pale, accentuated by the ever-popular black clothes, and whose body would be super-thin even without the three or four visits she makes to the gym each week. She has a great sense of humour and, as long as we keep the conversation light-hearted and jokey, we can have a good time together. Over coffee she quizzed me about my new life and for a moment I forgot myself, launching into a serious rave about the joys of Cloud Farm, the simplicity of a stress-free life and the sense of honesty and peace that I now felt within myself. She was appalled at my tone and suggested I was becoming smug and tedious — that my monologue had the ring of a newly converted fundamentalist!

I mention this encounter because it gave me a sudden glimpse of myself as I might appear to others, and I wasn't comfortable with what I saw. I began writing this book for my own benefit, not necessarily for others to read, but now that it is to be published, I worry that in telling the story I might indeed appear smug, or worse, sanctimonious — that my enthusiasms and convictions might read as proselytising or persuasion.

I don't want to give the impression that this lifestyle is for everyone or to imply that a life of simplicity should be pursued by all. The lesson I've learned, and go on learning, is about being brave and true to yourself, about claiming the space and time for reflection so that you can know what you truly want then, when the opportunity arises, you can make it happen. It's about getting to that moment in your life 'when dreams won't allow their wings to be clipped', as it's put in Jack Body's opera about Rewi Alley.

Cloud Farm brought me to that 'moment' as it did Heather. She behaved quite out of character when she thrust herself forward the night of the dinner party and invited herself to visit. Later she overturned a lifetime of dedicated and cautious work patterns by throwing in a permanent job at the age of 50. But both times she felt compelled to act, knowing that the opportunity would be lost forever if she didn't seize it. She's never been disappointed with her decisions and neither have I with mine.

Heather and I find we leave the farm less and less and resent the time spent going to the city even for essential tasks. Few people there seem to understand how we can be satisfied with our simple and non-intellectual lives. By writing this book I have discovered some of the motivations and reasons driving me to change, though not all. It is the unpredictability of life at Cloud Farm now and in the future which keeps us pursuing a goal that hasn't fully manifested yet. We don't know any more than anyone else quite where we are going with Cloud Farm nor what its full potential is. But we are very much enjoying the journey and the challenges along the way and we've found that as long as we stay true to the integrity of the land, we don't seem to go wrong.

I want to end the story where I began, with my boss at the medical school. This is the man who seemed unable to understand why I was leaving my job, whose persona cracked momentarily when I first gave him the news and who, by his unsympathetic reaction, personified all that I had begun to resent in that environment. I don't really know that I can take any credit, but I like to think that my news that day and the shock it caused made a slight chink in his armour. Last year, while still in his fifties and much to the surprise of his own bosses, he took early retirement to pursue a life of more meaning and less stress. I wish him all the best!

Historical note

The high tops above Akaroa where Cloud Farm sits are known by Maori as *Otepatatu* and are believed to be the home of *patupaiarehe* or Maori fairies, and of a race of wild men thought to be enchanted trees. There are stories of encounters with these fairy folk in both Maori and early Pakeha histories. There seems no evidence that Maori ever had dwellings at this height (most *pa* on the peninsula are close to the shore), but there was a walking route along the ridge-line which linked one bay with another.

European settlement in the second half of the nineteenth century saw much of the peninsula cleared of its magnificent timber trees and the land sown in cocksfoot and other pasture grasses. After timber-milling, dairying became a major industry as did the growing of cocksfoot seed for use in other parts of the country.

The area we call 'Cloud Farm' was first developed as a separate farming property in 1896 when it was bought by Fred Keegan, a 27-year-old of Akaroa. The following year he built the farmhouse and in 1898 married Bessie Keast of Christchurch. It became their first home where Bessie had her two children, Elsie in 1899 and Reg in 1903. It is not clear whether the farm was ever developed as a stand-alone economic unit, for Fred, who was a talented bullock-driver, seems to have spent a lot of his time working as such around Akaroa and the bays. Perhaps Bessie kept the farm going and Fred supplemented their income with his driving, while the land provided feed for the bullocks, and later horses, which were the mainstay of his business.

In any event, it seems that business went well, for some years later he bought land in the centre of Akaroa where he put up stabling for his animals and used the surrounding paddocks for their short-term grazing. In time he built an adjoining house and it seems that the family moved down there to live, retaining the farm purely as a grazing block for the animals. The farmhouse was occasionally let out to single men and farm labourers passing through the district.

The farm stayed in the Keegan family for 60 years until 1957 when it was sold to Leslie Harrington, a farmer of Takamatua, the adjacent valley. He continued to use the land just as a grazing block to supplement his own farm. The house was again rented out on an occasional basis and was known by then as 'Keegan's Cottage'.

Leslie Harrington owned the farm for 30 years and it was he who first recognised the unique beauty of its bush remnants and in 1986 took out a QEII National Trust Covenant to preserve them.

In 1987 the land was bought by Alison and Phil Bates, and her mother, Alice Moore. They worked very hard here, re-establishing natives and planting small sections in forestry and nut trees. Although they spent time in the house at weekends and on holidays, it was never their permanent home. In 1992 they took out a QEII covenant to protect a further 50 acres of regenerating bush.

They sold the farm in 1994 to a local company who began using it to graze cattle, but less than a year later it was on the market again, the owners not wanting to be constrained by the QEII conservation covenants. I bought it then, christening it 'Cloud Farm' in 1997, and have since extended the QEII covenant to cover all the ridge tops and alpine tussock areas.

I cannot say we've had any direct encounters with the fairies of Maori legend, but we've certainly felt their benign influence and they've surely contributed to the joyful times we've had here. Interestingly, one of the local farmers calls us the 'Fog Fairies' though it's probably more a commentary on our weather than reference to the legendary inhabitants!